SIX-FIGURE CHICKS

by

Mel Carr

CEO and Founder of Cloversy.com, an Executive Virtual Assistant Company, and Founder & Visionary of Six-Figure Chicks

Cloversy
Publishing

Published by Cloversy LLC DBA Cloversy Publishing. 7100 E Lincoln Dr., unit 3161, Scottsdale, AZ 85253. (480) 910-4111. www.Cloversy.com.

DISCLAIMER AND/OR LEGAL NOTICES

While all attempts have been made to verify the information provided in this book and its ancillary materials, neither the author nor the publisher assume any responsibility for errors, inaccuracies, or omissions and are not responsible for any financial loss by the customer in any manner. Any slights of people or organizations are unintentional. If advice concerning legal, financial, accounting, or related matters is needed, the services of a qualified professional should be sought. This book and its associated ancillary materials, including verbal and written training, is not intended for use as a source of legal, financial, or accounting advice. You should be aware of the various laws governing business transactions or other business practices in your particular geographical location.

EARNINGS & INCOME DISCLAIMER

With respect to the reliability, accuracy, timeliness, usefulness, adequacy, completeness, and/or suitability of the information provided in this book, Cloversy, LLC. make no warranties, guarantees, representations, or claims of any kind. Readers' results will vary depending on a number of factors. Any and all claims or representations as to income earnings are not to be considered as average earnings. Testimonials are not representative. This book and all products and services are for educational and informational purposes only. Use caution and seek the advice of qualified professionals. Check with your accountant, attorney, or professional advisor before acting on this or any information. Earnings potential is entirely dependent on the efforts, skills, and application of the individual person.

Any examples, stories, reference, or case studies are for illustrative purposes only and should not be interpreted as testimonies and/or examples of what reader and/or consumers can generally expect from the information. Any statements, strategies, concepts, techniques, exercises, and ideas in the information and materials offered are simply opinion or experience, and thus should not be misinterpreted as promises, typical results, or guarantees (expressed or implied). This book is provided "as is" and without warranties.

ISBN: 979-8-9871985-1-3

Printed in the United States of America

Dedication

Special Thanks to:

This book is dedicated to all the women who aspire to go further in their lives, whether by reaching that six-figure career milestone or scaling their own successful business.

Special thanks to the incredible women in my life who mentor and support me along the way. Your wisdom and guidance have been invaluable.

A heartfelt thank you to the female authors in each of these volumes, who bravely share their stories of success, the roadblocks they've overcome, and their secrets to living a profitable life. Together, we are proving that success is within reach for every woman who dares to dream big.

Special thanks to Kristen Hugens for her diligent editing and contribution as a ghostwriter for several chapters. You can find out more about her work at JoyfullCommunications.com. Also, heartfelt appreciation goes to Katrina Sawa for her expert marketing skills and her expertise in book editing, both of which were instrumental in catapulting Six-Figure Chicks, Phoenix, to #1 International Best-Seller status. Learn more about her services at www.JumpstartYourBizNow.com.

Table of Contents

SECTION 2

SECTION 3

I saw that six-figure women have two specific types of support that underearners seemed to lack—True Believers, people who recognize their potential and offer encouragement, and Way Showers, people who provide the map and serve as proof that success is possible.

- BARBARA STANNY,
Secrets of Six-Figure Women

Introduction

Six-Figure Chicks is a book that will inspire and motivate you to achieve more success than you can imagine!

What do we mean by "Six-Figure Chicks," exactly?

Yep, you guessed it...we make $100,000 OR MORE every year as business owners or in our careers.

Why did we create a book about good habits and stories from women earning six figures or more?

Because isn't that what everyone wants?

Well, it may or may not be what you think you want now, but it's absolutely possible!

And we're not talking about working our tails off while earning this income, either. While some of us DID do just that along the way, we eventually figured out how to do it without killing ourselves.

The goal of this book is to show you how to make a six-figure income (or more!) without killing yourself in the process—because NO ONE wants that.

Unfortunately, many women think that's what's required for financial success. Maybe you grew up with the mindset that in order to make more money, you have to work harder or put in longer hours at what you do.

The women who share their stories and strategies in this book are proof that it is possible to achieve great things, no matter where you come from or what your circumstances may be—and no matter what mindset you grew up with.

These women have all agreed to be a part of this book with me to "lift as we climb," bringing other women up with us. They are all hyper-focused on women achieving more, with more confidence and self-assurance than ever. We all want you to build a six-figure career or business with more ease, grace, and balance. YES, it IS possible to do that!

Who am I, and why did I create this concept?

When I started Cloversy, I never imagined the incredible journey it would take me on. My passion was simple: to give back time to entrepreneurs like me, so they could scale their businesses and focus on what they do best. In doing so, I also found immense joy in providing meaningful work opportunities to women across the United States. Cloversy became not just a business but a mission—to empower others to reach their full potential while creating a supportive environment for women to thrive.

As Cloversy grew, so did another dream: the Six-Figure Chicks brand. What began with a single book in 2022 has since blossomed into an empire, now launching its second book with many more to come. The Six-Figure Chicks movement is more than just a collection of stories; it's a beacon of inspiration, offering not just books but also merchandise and countless exciting ventures on the horizon. I am beyond blessed to witness this growth—something I never could have imagined when I first started out.

The Six-Figure Chicks featured in this book are living proof that success is within reach for every woman. Each of these incredible women has overcome obstacles, defied the odds, and achieved remarkable success in their fields. They have faced challenges head-on, turned setbacks into opportunities, and emerged stronger. Now, they share their stories with you, hoping to inspire and empower you to take your next step, no matter where you are in your journey.

We are women from diverse backgrounds, industries, and experiences, but we all share one common thread: we are six-figure chicks. Through our "How we got here" stories, we aim to provide you with the insights and lessons we've learned along the way. From goal setting and networking to mastering work/life balance and spirituality, our advice is here to help you fast-track your success.

Whether you're just beginning your career or you're already well on your way, this book is for you. The wisdom and experiences shared within these pages are designed to motivate you, challenge you, and push you toward achieving your own six-figure success.

So, what are you waiting for? Dive in and get ready to be inspired!

SIX-FIGURE CHICKS

Section 1

Our Stories, How We Got Here, and How to Connect with Us

In the first part of this book, you will get to read each author's story on how they got where they are now–in business, in their careers–and how they made it to Six-Figure Chick status. It's an introduction to the authors and their stories, how they grew their businesses and made it to six figures, so you can get to know them on a deeper level.

Amber Harman's *Story*

My mother had me at an extremely young age of seventeen in a German hospital. She is German, and all of our family resided in Germany; my biological father was in the military. We moved to the states when I was six where I got to spend a ton of time with my grandfather and grandmother (Oma); she was my favorite person in the whole world.

Due to the military life, we moved around a lot—always new schools and the hard life of being the new kid. I think my mom felt a little robbed of her childhood having my sister and I at such a young age, which did not make my relationship with her very easy.

My biological dad was out of the picture by the time I was eight, and my stepdad was also in the military. His career path took us all over the U.S.—to Dallas, Seattle, and then finally he ended up with his dream job with Southwest Airlines in Houston. This would be where my sister and I got to finish high school.

We lived in a very strict household, and we both moved out around the age of sixteen. I moved in with my best friend when I left; I was so grateful her mother took me in and treated me like her own daughter. When my sister left home, she moved in with her boyfriend, who she is still happily married to today.

Shortly after moving in with my best friend, I started dating her brother Scott. This caused major strain on our relationship. I lost my best friend and ended up getting my own place with Scott at the age of eighteen. I worked at a daycare and then started as a teacher's assistant at a learning center. I really enjoyed working with kids, but I still wasn't sure what I wanted to do with my life.

My mom also worked for Southwest in reservations, and I started feeling like maybe I should get my foot in the door. I wasn't sure what I wanted to do for Southwest; I just knew they had amazing benefits, and my mom and dad loved their jobs. So, I applied for every position I qualified for.

In case I wasn't accepted with Southwest, I also applied for nursing school at the same time. That meant I needed to apply for financial aid however, and when I went in to apply, they required I include my parents' income. This was ridiculous since I hadn't lived at home since I was sixteen. My only other option was to get married. I talked to Scott about it, and he agreed to go to the courthouse and get married. This made me eligible for financial aid.

In March of 2005, Southwest Airlines called me and offered me an interview for a flight attendant position. Being a flight attendant was nowhere in my plans, but it was Southwest! I was extremely nervous to interview, and I wasn't sure they were interested in me, but once I mentioned that my mom and dad both worked for the company, I WAS IN!

One night shortly after that, in April 2005, Scott went to an opening Astro's game with his co-workers. He called me to let me know his phone was going to die and not to worry.

He didn't come home on time or for hours thereafter. I went to the police station to see if anything had happened to him, and a female officer came out and told me there was a John Doe at the morgue that matched his description.

I was twenty-one years old with a dead husband. I was all alone again and at square one with no place to go.

A guy friend offered for me to stay with him, knowing I would be traveling most of the time. I was at such a low point in my life I didn't care anymore what happened to me. I was using drugs and had started to give up on life.

September 2005 came around, and I began my four weeks of flight attendant training. The training was in Dallas, Texas and it was insane with so much to learn, much more than I anticipated. I had to share a hotel room with a complete stranger and wasn't allowed to go home during those four weeks.

But training was free, my hotel room was provided for, and I was only responsible for meals. Once I passed all the tests and proficiencies I graduated and even got a check for $1000. I turned twenty-two years old in training, and I commuted to Baltimore for eight months until I finally got reassigned to Houston.

My roommate became my boyfriend (not the best decision looking back). Eventually I became pregnant, and we got married. He promised me the world: that he would stop using drugs, get a good job, and take care of us. I made the mistake of marrying the suitcase full of empty promises, and we divorced within months of my beautiful son being born. I decided my life and my choices were going to change because my child deserved the world, and I got my own place.

My mom was over the moon about her new grandson, so much so that she left Southwest to watch him while I flew. I am grateful for this, as she and I had an extremely strained relationship growing up. Having her for childcare came at an emotional cost for me, but it was free, and my son was happy and safe.

If it weren't for Southwest, I couldn't have been the single mom that I was. I never got any financial support from my son's father or his family. Southwest has provided me the freedom to move my days around. I can work as much or as little as I want. Our trips are generally three-day trips with four days off in between. I can give the trips away if I need to be there for my son, and I can pick up a trip last minute if I need more hours.

I have never missed anything that my son has needed me for. I made every game, every graduation, every appointment. I only missed some holidays when he was a baby. It is such a blessing to be able to make six figures and still be there for every single thing.

I'm not suggesting you run off and go work for Southwest, but it literally saved my life. The benefits are amazing. I get free health insurance, paid vacations, holiday pay, profit sharing, a 401k match of 9.3%, and I travel free, and so does my family. I get to see new places all the time and work with different crews almost every trip. I meet so many people.

The best part of my life was when I met my current husband, Rick. We met in 2015 when he volunteered to help with my son's Cub Scouts. We didn't connect then because he moved to Hawaii, but once Southwest started flying to Hawaii in 2019, we started hanging out more. The quick inter-island flights allowed him to meet me on my overnight stays. I had been single for so long and was so nervous, but I'm blessed that God pushed me hard and challenged me to trust again.

In March 2020, he proposed, and by December 2020, we were married. I finally have unconditional love and a man that is the most amazing father to my son.

My hope is that my story inspires you to keep going, keep reaching for more in your life and never settle. You deserve to be loved, respected and to earn more money too, even six-figures or more!

These days Rick and I have learned a lot about money wins and losses, and we have started working on wealth management solutions for individuals and families. We're excited about creating a more home-oriented type of lifestyle as traveling gets a little hard on you.

Favorite Quote

"Sometimes when you're in a dark place you think you've been buried, but you've actually been planted"

— CHRISTINE CAINE

Recommended Affirmation

Everything happens for a reason.

Amber's Special Offer

If you'd like to connect with me to hear more or talk with me about building wealth for your family, your journey and more, please reach out! You can contact me here: www.AmberHarman.com

About Amber Harman,

Flight Attendant

Amber Harman has been a flight attendant for the past twenty years. She enjoys the perks of traveling the world and meeting many people. The job provides a service to passengers but also requires training for medical situations and emergencies on the aircraft. This flexibility allows her to work and allows her to be a good mom and wife.

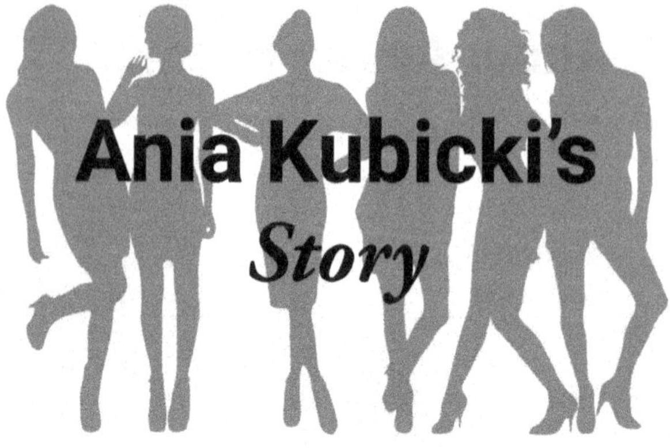

Ania Kubicki's *Story*

Spring 2024. I was pitching yet another 'crazy' idea to a friend. Instead of the usual skepticism, my friend grinned and said, "I just can't wait to see what you're going to do next!"

That stopped me in my tracks. "Am I really that interesting?" I laughed. But it made me think.

My life has always been a thrill ride. I've lived by the motto, "If my life were a movie, I'd want to watch it on the edge of my seat." Indeed, it's been an adventure.

Steve Jobs nailed it: "You can't connect the dots looking forward; you can only connect them looking backward." Now, sitting in my office at the Center for Positive Media, as CEO of ANGLES Communications, juggling international clients and championing select causes, I see how true that is. I never saw this coming.

Looking back, my journey from a non-English-speaking teenager in Stamford, CT, to the helm of a thriving communications firm was anything but predictable.

I moved to the U.S. in the summer of 1988, leaving behind a Europe on the brink of seismic change. The Berlin Wall was about to fall, and Poland was the epicenter of political turmoil. I didn't know much about the American life, except that it was an amazing opportunity. I wasn't the first one in my family. My great-grandfather had immigrated to the U.S. in the late 1800s, and I felt blessed to continue his dream. Every new place I see, every city I visit, and every road I discover, I feel his presence, sharing the journey through my eyes.

Entering an American high school in Stamford, CT, without a word of English or a clue about trends was a crash course in survival. Clothing brands, hairstyles, slang—I knew none of it. Sink or swim, and I chose to swim. Fast forward: four grueling years but I graduated early with honors, early acceptance to a university of my choice, and enough AP credits to leave early and return to Poland to finish high school there too. In college, majoring in political science, I hoped to change the world but soon realized a political career was not for me. The more I delved into it, the more out of place I felt. I graduated feeling lost and slightly depressed, with one certainty: politics was not my future.

Before the internet, finding a job meant navigating job agencies, and I needed work. New York was my target, and the Chrysler Building was my dream. I didn't care what I did (as long as it wasn't politics), I just wanted that iconic zip code. I applied for an executive assistant position at an investor relations firm. I nailed the interview and spent the next year on the 32nd floor of my favorite Art Deco building with the majestic eagles perched outside my window. It was pure magic.

During my review, my boss asked, "What do you like the most about working here?" Without missing a beat, I told him I loved watching how the quarterly earnings press releases could make or break stock values. My boss nodded and said, "Funny, you never thought about working in PR." Uh, what? That one question changed my career trajectory. It was the start of my journey.

For the next few months, I devoured every PR book I could find at the NY Public Library. "Why didn't anyone tell me this field existed?"

I wondered. It was everything I wanted: influencing public opinion, communicating across the masses, all for good causes and good people. I knew instantly that I was meant for PR, but I had no clue how to break in.

I scoured the NYT job postings, and on one fateful Metro-North ride, I found a listing for a public relations officer at the Polish Tourism Board. It required bilingual skills, which I had, and experience, which I didn't—but I was undeterred. I figured I could translate my existing skills and enthusiasm into this role.

I remember sitting in that interview and boldly declaring, "I know I'm meant to do this." Maybe it was sheer confidence, or maybe the universe really does conspire to help you when you believe in something. My boss was intrigued enough to give me a trial period. I aced it and landed the job.

I was in heaven, running press trips to Poland, working with the media to promote my country as a top tourist destination. But I quickly realized there was a lot about PR I didn't know, and I lacked a mentor. Then, I discovered something astonishing: people had agency jobs in PR. They got to work on diverse accounts and do PR for a variety of clients. I was mesmerized by this premise. A whole new world opened up before me, and I thought, "This is where I belong—working for a variety of clients, thriving in the dynamic world of PR."

I started networking and within a couple of months landed a job at a boutique PR firm on Lexington Avenue that specialized in EU projects and other cool European initiatives. I found amazing mentors who took me under their wing. Through their guidance and dealing with the day-to-day operations, I learned so much about the business of PR. It was the perfect mentorship to secure my knowledge, refine my skillset, and as a result, I was soon recruited to work for one of the largest PR agencies that specialized in travel and tourism.

There, in my swanky 3rd Avenue office, with a window that often disappeared into the clouds, I overlooked iconic landmarks. It was a dream come true. I worked on massive campaigns for Atlantis, Sun International, and countries like South Africa and Jamaica. I traveled, worked hard, and was relentless. It felt like living in a sitcom episode (minus the drinking and questionable dating choices). I always had way too much work for that.

Then I got recruited by another agency and felt the itch to expand into the B2B world. So, I took a job as a new business development director and, along the way, met a guy I really liked.

But after the traumatic events of 9/11, New York felt different. Since my boyfriend and I were talking about marriage, we decided that moving to a new market was our chance for a better life. When an opportunity in Arizona opened, we jumped. I had never lived anywhere like Arizona before. Landing a job with one of the biggest agencies in Scottsdale, I worked on just about every real estate developer project you could imagine. It was amazing. I felt like I had stepped into a whole new world, one with massive saguaros instead of skyscrapers.

In 2004, our son was born. I thought I'd be okay with daycare, but I wasn't. With no family nearby to help and daycare being the only option, it was a tough spot. We were a two-income family, and my paycheck was essential. Plus, I truly loved my work.

When the short maternity leave was up, I remember calling my boss in tears, not knowing what to do. "It's the hardest decision that women have to make," he said. He was supportive and suggested I stay home longer to care for my baby. "I just want to make it till he's old enough to sit up by himself," I said through tears.

He understood and offered me freelance projects. This was before working from home was socially acceptable. Encouraged by this development, I reached out to all my former bosses and asked if I could freelance for them. To my surprise, every single one of them came back with assignments. Now I was busy, and work was heating up. I didn't know this was the unofficial start of my agency.

I always wanted a business but never had the guts, savings, or a clue to start one. Back when I worked in NYC, my daily train commute served as my classroom. I once spent my entire paycheck on a Tony Robbins program. His voice in my headset became my mentor, transforming my life. With a notebook in hand, I mapped out my plans and dreams. Having a business was on that list. I just never imagined how I'd get there.

Yet, driven by the desire to create a better life for my son, I moved mountains. ANGLES was officially born when my son turned two.

By 2007, I had five employees, served on prestigious boards, joined leadership programs, made AZ Business Magazine's "35 under 35," and even landed a Business Journal cover. Happy team, happy clients, bigger office. Then, the 2008 market crash hit.

I naively thought I was safe because my clients weren't all in real estate. Wrong. Budgets were cut, and I had to let my team go. Thinking back to that shrinking office, team, and bank account, it feels like a bad movie. It was devastating, and I still have nightmares about it.

It took me ages to decide if and how I wanted to rebuild. I eventually opted for a smaller, leaner operation—three to four people max. And we stayed tight and efficient.

Then Covid hit. Cue the panic! But soon, I realized that in a crisis, communications are everything. The need for our services skyrocketed. By 2022, I moved my office into the Center for Positive Media, surrounded by some of the Valley's top media personalities. We're all about shifting the narrative to tell great, uplifting stories. And the work? It keeps flowing in. I am blessed with amazing clients, projects, and ideas. ANGLES keeps me connected to the community, through organizations like NAWBO and PRSA.

But then came the ultimate passion project: I was invited to be one of the co-founders of The Love Tower. Imagine a place dedicated to love, compassion, and positive change. The Love Tower's mission is to create a better world through acts of kindness, community engagement, and support for those in need. This work gives me a sense of purpose and fulfillment that goes beyond professional success.

I also dove into a new project altogether. Enter: Lagree. This fitness regimen swept me off my feet, transformed my body and made me feel so strong that I decided to document my journey. I call it My Mega Adventures (thanks to the Megaformer we use for Lagree exercises). It's a creative outlet and a gift to myself for my 50th birthday, which I will celebrate in December 2024. You can follow this journey with me on Instagram @MyMegaAdventures.

Reflecting on my life's twists and turns, my path is paved with gratitude. With my son off to college and the support of amazing people around me, I now have the freedom to explore new horizons. I work hard, work out even harder, and travel. Because without interesting days, what stories would we have to tell?

Here's the advice I give my son, and now to you:

- **Surround yourself with positivity and ambition.** We are the sum of the five people we spend the most time with, so choose wisely.
- **Focus on positive language.** Instead of saying, "I don't want to fail," say, "I want to succeed." The brain struggles to process negatives. When we say, "I don't want this," the brain ignores the "don't" and focuses on "want this," often bringing about what we are trying to avoid. Instead, focus on what is desired.

- **Align your thoughts, words, and actions.** You are a co-creator of your reality.
- **Embrace the winding paths.** You can only connect the dots looking backward.

So, remember that phrase my friend said that stopped me in my tracks? Let me end this by being that voice that says: "Hey, you! I can't wait to see what you're going to do next!" Then go out there, do your thing and be that voice for someone else.

Favorite Quote

"Don't take anything personally. Nothing others do is because of you. What others say and do is a projection of their own reality, their own dream. When you are immune to the opinions and actions of others, you won't be the victim of needless suffering."

– MIGUEL RUIZ,
The Four Agreements

Recommended Affirmation

I live my life as if everything was rigged in my favor. I embrace each adventure with gratitude, and let love guide my way.

Ania's Special Offer

Ania Kubicki is the founder of ANGLES Communications, a Phoenix based PR agency. She is one of the co-founders of The Love Tower at Ashah. Her passion project is My Mega Adventures where she channels her passion for wellness and travel into fun docuseries.

About Ania Kubicki,

CEO Angels Communications

Ania Kubicki is the founder of ANGLES Communications, where she connects visionary ideas with impactful audiences. With over 25 years of experience, Ania specializes in designing communications programs that drive positive change. She served as the 2022 President of NAWBO Phoenix and co-chaired the 2022 Trends Charitable Trust Gala. Ania's expertise spans corporate communications, public relations, and community outreach, making her a recognized leader in her field.

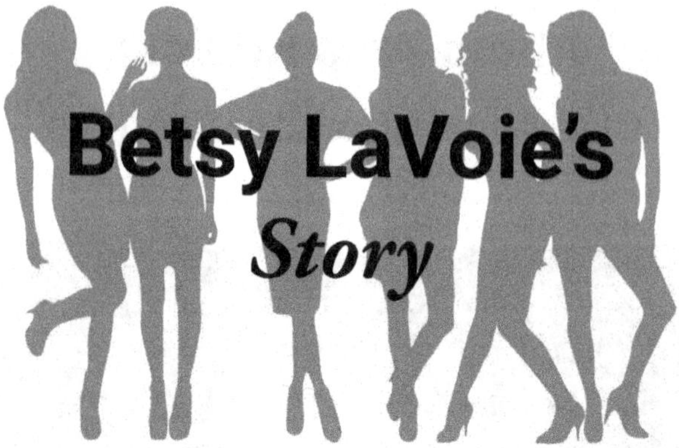

Betsy LaVoie's *Story*

The journey is not the destination. Growing up I watched adults change their careers multiple times. I was nervous for that to be me because, at the time, I felt like I needed to know what I wanted to do and be when I grew up.

In reality, it was in *my journey*, that I discovered what I was truly meant to do AND what brought me to being a Six-Figure Chick!

As a sixteen-year-old I saw a chiropractor after a minor car crash, who in my eyes was very transformative—not only physically but also intellectually regarding how I viewed health and the body. This chiropractor affected me so positively, I decided I wanted to be a chiropractor when I grew up.

The concept to heal thy body naturally remains strong within me today however the path to becoming a Chiropractor was quickly squashed in college with the realization that Chemistry and I were not compatible.

Transitioning to a Bachelor of Arts degree in Spanish seemed like the logical next choice since I had many credits towards that degree already. Plus, I got to take a semester abroad at the University of Guadalajara, an opportunity I was thrilled to embark on.

Still not having found the "destination" quite yet... I was thoroughly enjoying the journey...

Newly graduated and newly married, I decided to try owning my own Direct Sales Marketing business with Mary Kay Cosmetics.

Within fifteen years, this Type A personality girl landed five company cars, was in the top 1.5 percent of the company, AND was doing this in a very small town, I might add!

I also had my Realtor's license as my dad and brother were in the building industry, and they needed someone else in the family to be in real estate when my mom retired. I hung my license locally and remained active solely for the sake of family for ten years.

But with the birth of my second child, I decided it was time for a change.

Because of the success I had achieved in my journey with Mary Kay, almost everyone I knew thought I was nuts to give it all up. I, however, knew it was time for a change and didn't mind not knowing exactly what that change would be.

Alas, another leg in my journey continues... Following my heart and intuition while knowing there was something more for me.

Through my Mary Kay career, I learned to speak professionally in front of crowds of 500 or more. I learned how to overcome sales objections... a skill every person should have the privilege to learn. You use these skills throughout every profession and relationship we all experience!

In fifteen years, I created a team of thousands of salespeople and thousands of clients. I learned budgeting, marketing, sales, retention, customer service, brand awareness and activation, networking, staff management, people management, and so much more.

That priceless training and thinking outside the box, led me to creating a Facebook Group called Fountain Hills Connection. As a resident of our town without a large marketing budget, I wanted to create a way for local businesses to advertise and promote themselves to one another.

What started as a media outlet for residents to become familiar with local commerce, turned into the largest media outlet in our town! I was literally "pounding the pavement" walking into stores and doors in our town to invite them to participate and post. It had also become a constant and consistent "unpaid" job that I had created for myself.

One of the businesses I walked into during my door-to-dooring was called Energy Oasis. I had seen it many times when taking my daughter to her dance class next door. Energy Oasis was a passion project by a local woman who, unfortunately, never became successful. In fact, she mentioned that she was interested in selling her business that day.

Before I knew it, combining my love of healing and business, I purchased Energy Oasis and rebranded it to eo2 Wellness and Oxygen Bar.

Similar to the quote: "How you do one thing is how you do everything," I went "all in" with this business. I moved it to a better location, and we were making a profit within that first year!

I really enjoyed taking a failing business that was run like a hobby and turning it into a viable successful business that was "sale-able" for 3.5 times the amount I purchased it for! So, I sold that business and found myself ready for a new adventure, a new work challenge.

You probably think, is this woman ever going to settle on one passion or career path? And when does she end up making six-figures? I'm getting to that...

The thing is though, the journey that I was on to GET to the destination of where I am today, is what truly matters.

So, on the next stage of my journey, I got the courage to start a new product business from scratch. You see, throughout my entire adult life, I had created my own paper planners because the ones in the stores just never lived up to what I needed or wanted. I was always using my own self-created planner. So, I embarked on launching my own planner company.

I started out with a Kickstarter campaign to create interest and pre-sales with the newly launched IMPACT Planner. My IMPACT Planner included a balanced approach to make the largest impact possible on entrepreneurial ventures, health, wealth, relationships, and spirituality.

The first Kickstarter fell short of the goal, however I learned there was definite interest, and I tried again. With a successful second launch, the new planner went to print. Unfortunately, the competition with China to produce a reasonably priced printed planner was challenging. That, combined with the death of my biggest cheerleader, my mother, caused me to decide to end production and pursue being a Realtor to pay homage to my mom.

While working successfully as a Realtor, raising 2 children, losing 120 pounds *(story for another book)* I continued to manage and monitor the Fountain Hills Connection Facebook group.

It was through this group that I first learned of a job posting in my town for a Sales Associate at the Fountain Hills Chamber of Commerce. The job description literally felt like it had been written specifically for me. It was the perfect role for me in a town I love, supporting and promoting local businesses which I was passionate about. The only hiccup was that the pay was a fraction of what I was currently earning as a Realtor, so I dismissed the post.

Over the next three months, I continually thought of that job opportunity and kept it in the back of my mind. Right before Christmas, all three of my real estate transactions fell apart, and as a single mom, I decided a fraction of my current pay that was consistent was better than nothing, so I applied for the job.

After nine weeks of interviews with the Chamber I was hired. I was able to maintain my real estate license just in case. I immediately dove into the role at the Chamber, and it was a perfect fit for me! Growing our Chamber membership numbers rapidly and supporting new and existing businesses locally was very rewarding for me.

Six weeks after I started that role, the Chamber's CEO and President resigned, and he encouraged me to apply for the CEO position, which I did! There were 108 other candidates that the Chamber board sifted through over a period of two months. It was grueling, and I wasn't sure if I'd land the position or not, but I did!

During my first year as CEO, the pandemic occurred, two of our four employees passed away, and we pivoted in many ways still serving our local businesses. However, through all of these obstacles, we thrived, and our Chamber has now reached a 206 percent increase in the time I have led.

I love what I do now, and just like I've done with every job or career path on my journey, I go "all in." I know or learn what it takes to make it a success. I continue learning and growing my expertise, my experiences and my connections.

I believe we all have our own journeys, whether a career path, a health or healing journey, a relationship journey or other. We have to live that journey to our fullest in order to create the life we're meant for and one that brings us the most joy and success.

Today, after five years as CEO and President of the Fountain Hills Chamber of Commerce, I have reached my destination... and achieved the goal of also being a Six-Figure Chick!

I still have other passions I'm excited to pursue. In fact, in writing this chapter, it's inspired me to write my own book about whole body wellness and my weight loss journey. I want to share with more women how to lose that weight and keep it off like I have.

I also plan to bring back my planner because it's still the best one out there in my opinion.

Keep pursuing your dreams and enjoy the journey!

Favorite Quote

"People are exactly where they deserve to be by the choices they have made or allowed others to make for them"

— EARL NIGHTINGALE

Recommended Affirmation

I can do anything I cannot do everything. I've got this!

Betsy's Special Offer

I'm not done, and if you would like to hear more from me, I would love to connect with you on Facebook, or go download the digital version of my professional planner I created called IMPACT planner online at www.SixFigureChicksBetsy.com.

About Betsy LaVoie,

CEO /President Fountain Hills Chamber of Commerce

Betsy LaVoie is the CEO and President of Fountain Hills Chamber of Commerce, Managing Director of Fountain Hills Chamber Foundation; a proud Fountain Hills resident since 1978, Betsy LaVoie has played an active role in the town's growth from 900 residents to a vibrant community. As CEO since 2019, she is passionate about promoting local businesses and fostering collaboration. Betsy's deep ties and extensive experience uniquely position her as a dedicated advocate for the success and prosperity of Fountain Hills.

Cassie Velasquez's and Robin O'Shea's *Story*

Cassie

The mantra: grow up, graduate from high school, go to college, get married, start a family. Isn't that what everyone does? That is what I thought based on how I was raised. Interestingly, there was never much emphasis on what I should focus on in college; it was just assumed in my family that you go to college. So that is what I did.

I grew up in Fargo, North Dakota, and I had a wonderful childhood. I have two older brothers that I adore and two parents that took very good care of me.

Growing up in the Midwest was a gift that I didn't realize until I moved to Arizona in the early 90's after I graduated from college. I thought that everyone knows their neighbors and talks to the person in front of them at the grocery store. I thought everyone leaves their doors unlocked, and everyone smiles and waves to those passing by. Once I left my bubble, I realized that is not necessarily the culture in other places.

When I went to college, I had no clue what I wanted to do. After meeting with a guidance counselor, he told me to pursue a degree in teaching, specifically teaching children with special needs. Teaching was never on my radar, but I grew up doing what I was told to do. So, that is what I did.

I graduated from college with a degree in teaching children with special needs, and since "get married" was the next step in the mantra, that is exactly what I did. I never once considered if the person I was marrying was the person that I wanted to spend the rest of my life with. As it turns out, he wasn't. It was then that I knew my thinking needed to change.

I moved to Scottsdale, Arizona to pursue a job in teaching. I really loved the job because I loved helping children and I loved their families. Fast forward to 2003. This was a bittersweet year. The sweet part was I found and married a wonderful man with whom I just celebrated twenty years of marriage. We have two beautiful, healthy boys that are thriving. I have been very blessed in my life and for that, I am grateful. The bitter part was I lost my mom to cancer at the age of fifty-nine. This was another indication to me that life is too short to just follow a mantra.

I ended up teaching special education for fifteen years. Although teaching was not something that I grew up wanting to do, I put my all into it. I was nominated for teacher of the year in 2003, as well as obtained my real estate license, started a summer program at my school and earned a master's degree in education. But after fifteen years, the mantra kicked back in, and I remembered that the next step was to start a family. So, I retired from teaching in order to stay home and take care of my boys. During this time, I continued to work part time in the school district, and I also taught online classes at a local university.

Once my boys went to kindergarten, I thought, "Now what?" Remember, there was nothing in the mantra after 'start a family.' It was time to think about what I was going to do next, and I knew that I wanted to do something different. This is when I met Robin and *Cassobin* was born.

Robin

Driven, goal-oriented, ambitious, enterprising...these are words that jump out at me when thinking about how I would describe myself. Even from a very young age, I knew if I wanted something it would only require some thought, a solid plan, and action!

I grew up in Scottsdale, Arizona, in a loving family with one sister and two caring, hard-working parents. My dad was an airline pilot, and my mom stayed home with us until we were old enough to take care of ourselves after school. We were fortunate to have a supportive, safe, and comfortable childhood with lots of opportunities to travel, learn, and play.

With that being said, when my sister and I wanted something special it was expected that we would work to earn it. Having a strong work ethic was expected and highly valued in our family.

When I wanted a new toy, or to go to the roller-rink I knew the way to get there was to sell old toys at a family garage sale and run many, many lemonade stands. But as my wants increased, I discovered the real money came from extra chores around the house and miscellaneous jobs for the neighbors. I'll never forget the summer when I mucked out the neighbor's horse stalls in 115° heat. I couldn't wait to be a few years older and be allowed to babysit like my sister...she always seemed to get the easy gigs!

Of course, I also learned that making money wasn't the only step in getting the coveted prize. My earliest realization of this was when I was ten years old and wanted to buy the neighbor's pet rabbit. After asking permission, my parents told me to find out what that would entail. So, I interviewed the neighbor and called the local pet store for specifics on what I would need to take care of a rabbit and how much it would cost. I wrote everything down and then created an earning plan to get to my goal. I then presented it to my parents, and we mapped out a reasonable timeline. In the end, I did get "Marshmallow," the rabbit. But the true reward was the pride I felt in planning and earning him!

That experience taught me that setting goals with a specific plan for how to achieve them was a fail-safe way to get exactly what I wanted! To this day, the process informs all my financial, personal, and professional decisions.

After graduating from college, I had the opportunity to move to Ireland. I had planned to go to law school, but when this opportunity crossed my path, I knew I could not pass it up! The year in Ireland proved to be a pivotal change in my journey. Unfortunately, I did not have a work visa so my plan for employment in a "solicitor's office" didn't quite work out. So instead, I knocked on doors, talked to anyone who would listen, and ended up finding a job at a school for adults and children with disabilities...my whole world opened up. I loved working and interacting with the students whose eyes would light up every time they learned something new or had a new experience. Every day was an adventure in creating new opportunities for them. It also fulfilled my desire to advocate for people typically marginalized by society (my law school dream).

The time spent in Ireland was a wonderful year filled with new friends, new experiences, and lots of travel. After the year ended, I returned home and went back to school for a master's degree in special education. I now knew my calling. Over the next twenty-five years, I would set and achieve new professional goals moving from classroom teacher to educational specialist and finally an administrator. I especially enjoyed working with staff and families to help bridge the gap between home and school. This is how I met Cassie and Cassobin was born.

CASSOBIN

Have you ever had an attraction to someone so strong you felt the universe played a part in bringing you together? Working in the same school district and teaching at Grand Canyon University together had made us friendly acquaintances. We had worked together for years but had never really spent time together socially, but we always knew we wanted to get to know each other better.

That is when a training called *IEP Facilitation* came across our desks. Little did we know, we both thought the training sounded interesting. So independently we both signed up. Walking into the training and seeing each other was like lightning had struck! In fact, we immediately started rearranging the room (and the seated participants) so that we could sit next to each other! When we were asked to write our names on our name cards, Robin wrote "Awesome", and Cassie wrote "Beautiful." The fun had begun.

What we didn't expect was that over the next three days, our lives would change both professionally and personally. The training content and approach were incredible. By the end of the first day of training, we were both thinking, "Where has this information been all of our lives?" That night, we each went home excited to share with our families what we were learning and how we could use the information to change IEP meeting experiences for families and staff members.

Cassie's husband, Brian, gave us even more food for thought when he said, "Think bigger."

After the second day of the training, we took the owners of the company to happy hour, and as it turned out they were looking for trainers. For the next few years, we had the time of our lives juggling our careers and family, traveling across the country, and training a curriculum that we both believed in and wanted to teach to others.

After a few years, the owners saw our enthusiasm and dedication and it prompted them to fly to Arizona to take us and our families to dinner and talk about a long-term partnership where ultimately, we would own the company when they were ready to retire. We were thrilled! Little by little we added more responsibility and managerial tasks to our plates and ultimately decided to take a leap of faith and retire early from the school system to work with the company full-time. Our new goal was to learn how to run the company and expand the business! During this time, we both went back to school to expand our knowledge. Cassie pursued another master's degree, this time focusing on dispute resolution, and Robin earned her Ph.D. in School and Family Partnerships.

Each year, setting and achieving expansion goals grew our business and financial success. In March of 2020, when the world shut down due to the pandemic, we kicked into high gear. With the inability to travel, we knew in order to keep the company alive we needed to do something...and fast. In true "Cassobin" fashion, we told the owners that we wanted to spend this time at home packaging the curriculum for delivery online. This turned out to be a wise decision as we were able to offer new virtual solutions to families and school staff. Once the world opened up again, travel picked back up, and our online trainings continued to thrive.

In 2022, after a year of negotiations, we bought the company. Within the first year, we doubled our profit margin! This was all due to intense planning and hard work, but it has been a blast because we have done it as best friends. Owning a business with your best friend is a gift and one that we do not take for granted. It does not come without challenges, but with open communication, trust, and love, we know that we can accomplish anything we put our minds to. Our mantra now: work hard, play hard and wake up every day with a grateful heart.

Favorite Quote

Work hard, play hard, dream big, love loads, laugh as much as you can, and give back

— DEIRDRE O'KANE

Recommended Affirmation

I am an honorable person who is truly grateful for the opportunity life has given me.

— CASSIE

I am a beautiful, unique soul, and I acknowledge that my existence and contribution on this planet are needed.

— ROBIN

Special Offer

As a thank you to Six-Figure Chicks readers, enjoy a **FREE FIEP training seat** ($480 value) and our **Communication Resource Sheet** to enhance your meetings. Fill out the form below, use code "SIX FIGURE," and download your resource sheet www.key2ed.com/six-figure-chicks/

About Cassie Velasquez & Robin O'Shea,

Co-Owner Key2Ed, Inc.

Cassie Velasquez, M.Ed., M.D.R., is co-owner of Key2Ed, an educational consulting company specializing in improving school and family partnerships. Cassie has over 30 years of educational experience in special education and is a national public speaker. She delivers professional development workshops to educators nationwide. With a master's degree in special education and a master's degree in Dispute Resolution, as well as being a certified mediator, she brings expertise to the field of special education related to conflict prevention.

Robin O'Shea, Ph.D., is co-owner of Key2Ed, an educational consulting company specializing in improving school and family partnerships. As a national speaker she presents on a variety of topics related to IEP Facilitation, Conflict Prevention and Resolution, and Family-Professional Partnerships. Robin has over 30 years of experience in the field of special education. As an IEP meeting facilitator and certified mediator, she brings real life experiences and scenarios to her training participants.

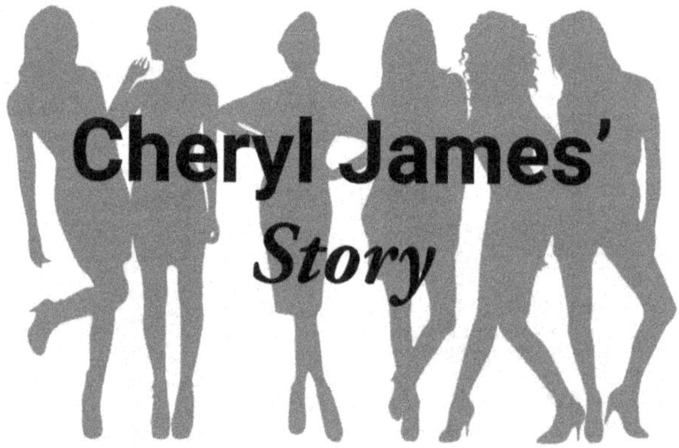

Cheryl James' *Story*

For nearly three decades, I was a corporate soldier, meticulously following the rules and climbing the ranks. As Senior Director of Operations and Product Development at a Fortune 100 company, I wore my title like a badge of honor. I developed global systems and consulted for some of the world's largest clients. Being a Black woman in leadership was a point of immense pride, especially in an environment where few people of color held director-level positions. Excellence was my obsession - I poured every ounce of my being into each project.

Yet the higher I climbed, the more I noticed the facade cracking. Endless meetings, corporate politics, and a nagging sense that my work, despite its importance, wasn't fulfilling me the way I had hoped. It felt like running a marathon with no finish line in sight. I often found myself wondering, "Is this it? Is this what success is supposed to feel like?"

Then came the wake-up call. I was tired of long hours, relentless stress, and doing things that didn't always sit well with me. George Floyd's tragic death was the straw that broke the camel's back. The company's response was a brutal reminder that, despite my years of dedication, I was just another cog in the machine. This stark realization hit me like a ton of bricks. I was done being a corporate drone. It was time for a change.

The decision was cemented during a grueling week when I juggled multiple high-stakes projects. I remember sitting in a boardroom, surrounded by executives more concerned with quarterly profits than the human cost of their decisions. I felt a profound sense of disconnection. It was as if I had been living someone else's life, following a script that no longer resonated with my values.

Deciding to leave a company where I had spent nearly three decades felt like ripping off a Band-Aid: fast, painful, but ultimately necessary. I knew I needed a plan, so I hired a business coach. That was one of the best decisions I've ever made. My coach was instrumental in helping me navigate this significant career shift and launch my own consulting business.

The process was daunting and filled with uncertainty, but it was also incredibly liberating. I remember the first few weeks vividly. There were moments of sheer panic mixed with exhilarating freedom: no more corporate jargon or endless emails about inconsequential things. Instead, I was drafting the blueprint for my future that aligned with my passions and values. I was stepping into the unknown but ready to embrace whatever came my way.

Those initial months were a whirlwind of self-discovery. I had to confront my deepest fears and insecurities - the nagging doubts buried under years of corporate conditioning. Was I really cut out for this? Could I make it on my own? With the support of my loved ones and an incredible therapist, I worked through the emotional turmoil of leaving my former identity behind.

Slowly but surely, a new sense of purpose began to take shape...

I founded my consulting business with a clear mission: to serve overwhelmed and burned-out female service-based business owners.

During my corporate tenure, I saw how big companies thrived with abundant resources. In contrast, small businesses often struggle to manage their money, resources, and tools effectively. I wanted to bridge that gap and bring my expertise to those who needed it most.

To understand my target audience, I spoke with numerous small business owners. They poured their hearts out, sharing their pain points and what they wished they had to make their businesses more efficient and successful. With this invaluable insight, I set out to provide clarity on operations, teaching my clients how to be more efficient, leverage systems and tools, and drive a positive customer journey.

One of my first clients was a talented event planner who was struggling to scale her business. She had a vision for creating luxury events but needed more operational know-how to bring her ideas to life efficiently. We worked together to streamline her processes, implement automation tools, and develop a comprehensive customer journey. The transformation was incredible. She went from feeling overwhelmed and burned out to confidently managing multiple high-profile events with ease.

The impact of my work has been nothing short of transformative. I have helped clients produce luxury private events internationally, develop high-scale onboarding experiences, and organize successful conferences. The feedback from my clients has been overwhelmingly positive. They appreciate the clarity and efficiency that my consulting brings to their operations. Seeing their businesses thrive is incredibly rewarding.

One of the most fulfilling aspects of my new career is the freedom it affords me. I get to pick and choose the clients I work with, ensuring that I am passionate about each project. I have the time freedom to travel with my husband and enjoy afternoon lunches with friends. This balance between work and personal life has brought me immense peace and happiness.

Let's not sugarcoat it though; transitioning from corporate life was tough. Leaving behind a steady paycheck and the security of a well-defined role was terrifying. The early stages of my business were filled with doubts and sleepless nights. The stress of starting something new, coupled with the lingering effects of PTSD from my corporate days, made the transition even more challenging.

However, I found strength in my purpose and the support of my business coach and loved ones. One strategy that helped me cope was focusing on the positive impact I was making. Each success story and each client who expressed gratitude for my help reinforced my decision to leave corporate life. I also learned to prioritize self-care, ensuring I took time to relax and recharge. This balance was crucial in managing my PTSD and maintaining my mental health.

I vividly remember a particularly difficult day early on in my business. I had faced a series of setbacks, and the doubt was creeping in. But then, I received an email from a client. She wrote about how my advice had completely transformed her business, allowing her to spend more time with her family while still achieving her professional goals. That email was a lifeline. It reminded me why I had taken this leap of faith in the first place.

Walking away from a successful corporate career was one of the hardest decisions I have ever made, but it was also the best decision. Today, I am living my purpose, helping female entrepreneurs achieve their dreams and scale their businesses. The peace and fulfillment I have gained are immeasurable. I am no longer just a worker bee; I am a leader, a mentor, and a changemaker.

My perspective on work and success has changed dramatically. Success is no longer about climbing the corporate ladder or achieving a prestigious title. It is about making a meaningful impact, enjoying what I do, and having the freedom to live my life on my terms. While the path has been challenging, I wouldn't change a thing. This journey has taught me resilience, self-belief, and the power of following your heart's calling.

As I look to the future, my goal is to continue supporting and empowering female entrepreneurs. I plan to expand my consulting services and offer more comprehensive solutions to help my clients scale their businesses. I am also considering launching workshops and online courses to reach a broader audience and share the lessons I've learned.

The journey has been challenging, but it has also been incredibly rewarding. I am grateful for the experiences that led me here and am excited about the future. Walking away from corporate life was not just a career change but a transformation. I found my purpose, and in doing so, I found peace, fulfillment, and a new identity. This is just the beginning, and I am excited to see where this journey will take me next.

Favorite Quote

"Life isn't about finding yourself. Life is about creating yourself."
— GEORGE BERNARD SHAW

Recommended Affirmation

I have the power to change my story.

Cheryl's Special Offer

For readers of Cheryl James' chapter in ***Six-Figure Chicks Phoenix*** book, she is offering a special gift: Claim your free 90-minute Consulting Power Session! This personalized session is designed to help you break through barriers, find clarity, and create a strategic plan to get unstuck and achieve success and profitability. Whether you're struggling to scale your business, manage operational challenges, or simply want a fresh perspective, this session will provide actionable insights tailored to your unique situation. Don't miss this opportunity to work directly with someone who's been in your shoes and knows the path to success. www.sixfigurecheryl.com

About Cheryl James,

CEO/Founder, C L James Consulting, LLC

Cheryl James, founder of CL James Consulting, is a seasoned business strategist with 27 years of corporate experience, including leadership roles in global teams and product management. After turning 40, she launched her own venture to empower entrepreneurs. Specializing in digital marketing, project management, and operational efficiency, Cheryl helps businesses streamline operations and focus on growth. She's also a dedicated SCORE volunteer, passionate about helping others achieve success.

Ginger Clayton's *Story*

When I reflect on my journey to achieving mid-six figures, these key attributes come to mind: resilience, determination, innovation, creativity and a relentless pursuit of balancing both business leadership and community impact. I hope to show you through my story that you can achieve six-figure success while making a significant difference in the lives of others. By balancing ambition with compassion and always looking for ways to give back, you too can achieve this goal.

I had strong women in my life who were role models of these qualities. I was raised by a single mom in a small Vermont town, where people worked hard and were active parts of the community helping one another. My mom taught me that when things get tough, there's always someone in a tougher situation who we can help. This philosophy has guided my life and career. From an early age, I wanted to make a difference in my work. In high school, I volunteered on an ambulance crew. Negotiating chaotic situations, building trusting relationships and developing critical thinking skills were necessary components of my work. During my college years, I married and divorced, becoming a single mom working three jobs and taking classes. One morning, I realized I only had two diapers left and no money to buy more. With some help from my boss, the Diaper Bank of Southern Arizona in Tucson provided me with a package of diapers, an act of kindness that would stay with me throughout my life and would later inspire me to find a way to give back and pay it forward.

While in college I worked as a paramedic for Rural/Metro Ambulance, where my desire to excel and advance my career was rewarded and resulted in promotions into statewide senior leadership. Then I became the Director of Operations at The Martz Agency. Both of these careers equipped me with the skills needed to eventually manage my own business. Early in my career I was offered advice by an older male colleague who was watching me work seventy to eighty hours per week while balancing my family needs. "You can't have a successful career and a thriving family. You will have to pick one." My response was, "I am determined to figure it out, and I will."

In 2001, I married the love of my life, Joe Clayton, who owned a technology company. He asked me to join the business because I had business management expertise. This was just after 9/11 and the resulting economic downturn. We began to look for a way to help us pull out of this dip. As we blended our families and had children, there was an opportunity to take a leap, and start a commercial relocation business. I had watched companies move locations and had ideas for ways to create greater efficiencies. A comment by one of the IT clients going through a company move mentioned that "it would be great if you could handle both IT systems and moving services." This sparked a new path forward. Wouldn't it be great if people moving into a new space could be excited about the opportunity instead of stressed with the management of so many important aspects of the move?

It was definitely a challenging time to start a new company during the downturn. We went through many challenging months without pay, all the while investing every last dime into the company. We refinanced our cars and homes, putting everything on the line. I returned to using my single mom triple coupon system and serving "tuna pea wiggle." I was pregnant, with a toddler and three older kids.

Our business friends thought that we were crazy. We often heard, "What do a computer company and a moving company have to do with each other?" We had listened to our clients and believed we could provide services that would make our clients' lives easier. By offering a wider range of services we could meet so many relocation needs including: moving their office furniture, moving their IT systems, installing the low-voltage wiring (telephone and computer lines), VOIP telephone systems, and CCTV video surveillance systems, and providing card access and audio-visual needs for conference rooms. The risk was worth it with triple revenues in just the first year! Finally, no more tuna pea wiggle!

We ended up merging the businesses in 2005 and rebranded as Elontec, providing technology, relocation and telecommunication services. We had grown the relocation division and had a $1M contract providing furniture installation services for a furniture dealership. Around the time of the recession, a national company bought out that furniture dealer, resulting in them no longer needing us. We then had to figure out how to replace that revenue and ensure our employees' livelihoods. God works in mysterious ways as a client asked us to help remove multiple floors of furniture left behind by a company that went out of business. We obliged and started selling used and refurbished office furniture. Because we were no longer installing furniture for that company, we were now free to become a dealership ourselves. We chose a great US made furniture manufacturer as our flagship and added commercial furniture as one of the divisions.

Soon after, we were awarded a large statewide furniture contract, launching the beginning of our new office furniture division. Today, we provide commercial furniture, relocation, and technology solutions throughout Arizona and have a national contract installing furniture across the US. All of these services can be provided independent of one another or combined to provide the ultimate in efficiency for the major aspects of a corporate move.

In the beginning, I struggled to balance five children with our growing businesses. I am thankful as I reflect on the path my life has taken, the choices I made to be open-minded and flexible, to listen to the ideas of others and to be willing to take risks. I accepted the challenges I faced and stayed resolute in my plan to find a way to have it all. This took being humble, believing we could do it and developing the right strategies.

I followed the teachings from *The Seven Habits of Highly Effective People* by Stephen Covey, pinpointing my personal mission to create a 'fever to serve.' I defined my core roles—wife, mother, daughter, Christian, business leader, community servant—and created corresponding goals. By color-coding time spent in these roles in my Outlook calendar, I ensured I dedicated time to each role. One important lesson from this was my wife role, or 'blue time.' Joe commented that we didn't spend enough quality time together. I was sure he was wrong as we were together 24/7 between work and home. I looked at my calendar and there was no blue; he was right! I had been multitasking my time with him in work meetings, charity events, client dinners, kids' sports, etc. Without delay, we instituted a weekly date night, plus no work talk at home.

With my purpose to create a Fever to Serve, I started our ElonServe initiative, fostering a culture of giving back. We are all families helping families at the end of the day. Every employee is encouraged to serve the community with unlimited service hours and participate in our annual events. Serving on the boards of various non-profits has allowed me to form relationships with other business leaders and make a significant impact as well.

To scale the business, I meticulously tracked my time and activities, realizing I was too focused on daily operations instead of strategic growth. I categorized every task—accounting, HR, business development, marketing, operations—to determine what could be delegated. Was this task something that could be delegated or did it need to be done by me? What was the level of urgency and importance? Was it the best and highest use of my time? Assessing each task's urgency and importance, I identified where my efforts were best spent.

I found that 'thinking time' was crucial but often overshadowed by routine tasks. By analyzing the data, I saw the need to delegate accounting, purchasing, dispatch, and project management tasks. This shift allowed me to concentrate on strategy and growth. We then hired additional salespeople, an office manager, a controller, and an operations manager, facilitating our expansion.

I changed my mindset from working "in" the business to "on" the business. We went from having 20 employees and $3M in revenue, to 75 employees and over $20M in revenue by 2024, with continued growth projected.

My commitment to give back to my community and build from a kindness shown to me in 2013 led to the establishment of the Diaper Bank of Central Arizona. Our mission is to provide one million diapers to families in need, addressing a critical but often overlooked necessity. One small package of diapers given to me in a time of desperate need resulted in the distribution of over 10 million diapers to date. We ultimately merged the two diaper banks, creating the Arizona Diaper Bank helping statewide, where I now serve on the Board of Directors.

My story is a testament to how business success can pair with making a meaningful impact in the community. We survived the 9/11 downturn, the recession, and a pandemic. I have grown from being a young, struggling single mother to the CEO of a thriving company and founder of a crucial nonprofit. I have seen firsthand the profound influence one person can have. It has driven my determination, innovation, and compassion. My journey has been a relentless pursuit of business excellence and community impact.

With a solid team, Joe and I can now take bucket-list trips. We realized during Covid that life is too short to postpone dreams until retirement. Though it took time, I have found a way to balance being a loving wife, involved mom, dedicated friend, woman of faith, community servant, and business leader. I do have it all!

I hope my journey offers invaluable lessons and inspiration for those looking to achieve six-figure success while driving positive change.

Favorite Quote

"Use your fear... it can take you to the place where you store your courage."

— AMELIA EARHART

Recommended Affirmation

Adapt, improvise, overcome!

Ginger's Special Offer

As a special gift to readers, Ginger Clayton invites you to visit SixFigureGinger.com, where you'll find exclusive tips on creating a joyful office move, enhancing office ergonomics, and fostering a thriving workplace culture. Discover practical advice that can transform your work environment and help you lead with confidence and ease.

About Ginger Clayton,

CEO/President Elontec

Ginger, CEO of Elontec since 1997, is dedicated to helping others advance. Elontec, a leader in commercial furniture, moving, and technology solutions, has earned local and national recognition, including the ASU Spirit of Enterprise and Greater Phoenix Chamber IMPACT Awards. Ginger's commitment to community service is evident in her founding of the Diaper Bank of Central AZ in 2013, which has provided one million diapers 'annually' to families in need.

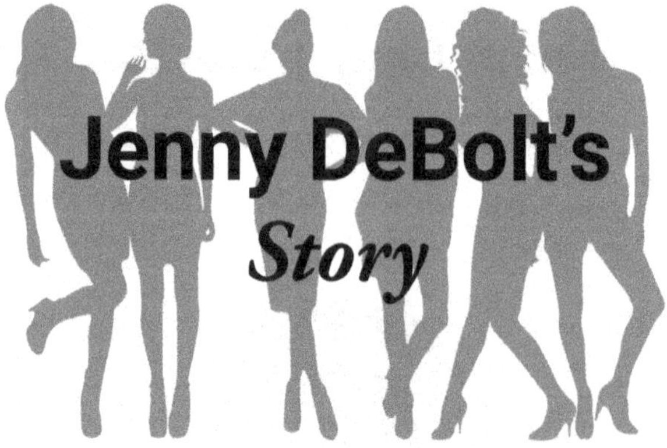

Jenny DeBolt's *Story*

Life has a peculiar way of throwing curveballs when you least expect them. One moment, you're riding the crest of a wave, confident in your position and accomplishments, and the next, you're struggling to stay afloat in the choppy waters of uncertainty. For me, that moment came when I was fired from a company where I was making a substantial amount of money and had built a multi-million-dollar division in a new venture for their brand. I had quite literally loaned my own personal brand to build theirs. There was no justifiable reason for letting me go, and a lot of secret underhanded planning going on to get it done. I was being betrayed by my own team to protect their jobs. How could they do this to me in this manner? How could something like this be done to someone that made a strong brand and a lot of money? Why would they do this to a good person? It felt like the rug had been pulled out from under me, and I was left grappling with a whirlwind of emotions.

The initial shock was paralyzing. I had dedicated years of hard work, always going above and beyond my duties. I had more than delivered on employment promises, to the amazement of the owner even. To be dismissed so abruptly felt like a personal attack, a rejection of my worth and contributions. Depression settled in quickly. The days seemed longer, and motivation became a distant memory. It wasn't just about the job; it was about my identity, my purpose.

In the depths of my despair, I realized I couldn't navigate this storm alone. I sought help, a decision that proved to be a lifeline. Therapy provided a safe space to unpack my emotions, confront my fears, and begin the healing process.

It was also during this time I read a book, ***Who's In Your Room***, that introduced a pivotal concept that would change my life: the importance of having a personal vision, mission, and values. We often hear about companies crafting their vision, mission, and values. These guiding principles shape their identity, drive their actions, and define their goals. But what about individuals? Why don't we apply the same framework to ourselves? This thought struck me like a bolt of lightning. If businesses could thrive with a clear sense of purpose, why couldn't I do the same for my life?

I immersed myself in literature on the subject, devouring reading materials both digitally and in print that explored the power of a personal vision, mission, and values. I learned that by establishing these guiding principles for oneself, one could navigate life's uncertainties with clarity and confidence. It was a revelation. For the first time in months, I felt a flicker of hope.

I took a step back and embarked on a journey of self-discovery. I asked myself tough questions: What did I want from life? What were my core values? What was my ultimate mission? It wasn't easy work while worn down, but it was necessary. Through introspection and reflection, I began to piece together my personal vision, mission, and values.

MISSION: A world where we all love each other for who and where we are now without judgment or expectations.

VISION: Make a memorable and lasting impact to make the world a better place.

MOTTO: Do the right thing and live the golden rule.

VALUES:

- God First
- Gratitude (always see the bright side)
- Positive Focus, Happy & Joyous Life
- Lead with Love, LUV, and Kindness (servitude)
- Be You
- You Come First
- Dream Big and Live Abundantly
- Be Confident and Courageous
- Be Mindful and Present
- Have Fun and Push the Limits
- Sequins Everyday (be the light for others)

Establishing these principles gave me a newfound sense of direction. They became my North Star, guiding my decisions and actions. With this clarity, I could face the future with more ease, knowing that my path was aligned with my deepest values and aspirations.

In addition to defining my vision, mission, and values, I also established deal breakers – non-negotiables that I would not compromise on, no matter the circumstances. These deal breakers ensured that my values remained intact and protected my mental and emotional well-being.

DEAL-BREAKERS:

- Not a Cheerleader for Others
- Negative Drama
- Rude/Disrespectful
- Lies/Steals
- Self-Absorbed/Narcissistic
- Runs with the Wrong Crowd
- Unreliable
- Cheater
- Abusive
- Judgmental/Racist/Bully/Superiority Complex

These deal breakers became my protective boundaries, helping me maintain my course and stay true to myself. They were a reminder that while external circumstances might be beyond my control, my response and choices were firmly within my grasp.

Embracing a personal vision, mission, and values transformed my life. It provided a framework for making decisions, setting goals, and navigating challenges. It empowered me to reclaim my identity and purpose, even in the face of adversity. Most importantly, it reminded me that my worth was not defined by my job or external achievements but by the values and principles I upheld.

After I was let go from that company, the very next day, I filed for my corporation to start my own commercial cleaning company due to the needed encouragement of my husband and a great friend. I was so nervous about it, but I knew myself well, so I knew I could do it. Inspired by the transformation in my personal life, I decided to apply the same principles to my company, Us Cleaning Solutions. I wanted my business to reflect the values I held dear and to operate with a clear sense of purpose. Having done this for myself personally, I had a great starting point to draw from.

VISION: Our Vision is to nurture loyal relationships with our clients, partners, and team members that stand the test of time who share our commitment to people, excellence, and a fun working environment.

MISSION: All of Us creatively working together to passionately clean and exceed expectations, transforming the perception of cleaning services from being a simple commodity to being a desired comfort with built-in, valued relationships. This comfort provides peace of mind and a delightful environment both physically and mentally.

SLOGAN: Connecting and Caring for People through Cleaning

VALUES: Our Values are:

- Faith in God and love of people
- Health of our culture and of people spiritually, mentally, and physically
- Dedication to our relationships
- Professionalism always
- Wisdom and creativity when seeking new innovative ways to clean
- Passion in pursuit of happiness and in cleaning solutions
- Recognition of things big and small to build people up

These guiding principles not only helped align my business operations with my personal values but also created a cohesive and motivated team. Everyone knows what we stand for and what we aim to achieve. It's not just about cleaning; it's about making a positive impact.

Fast forward six years from filing for my corporation, it is now a multimillion-dollar company quickly approaching $5M per year. Knowing who I am has broken personal limitations. It's been an amazing whirlwind navigating constant growth and, hence scaling. It's a non-stop journey of what I call 'good problems' to keep my frustrations in trying times in perspective, knowing they're a direct indicator that I'm blessed. Gratitude in all things!

Quick interesting side note, eight months after I was let go, someone from the company called to let me know that the reason I was let go was so a large personal purchase could be made by the owners. The reason I share this is perspective. My dismissal had nothing to do with my worth, and I was taking it very personally. Remember, other people's actions are not about you. YOU are amazing! Don't let anyone change your mind about that. They don't have a say in your worth. Ironically, being fired abruptly like that put a fire of perseverance in me and look where I am now. That rough period was one of the best things that has ever happened to me. I'm forever grateful for it now. It also taught me that my success doesn't have to be based on a consistent paycheck from a company. It wasn't even a secure job in hindsight, evident in my unjust dismissal. But now I have my own company and complete control over my prosperity.

I don't believe I could have come to all of those understandings without the deep dive into who I am, ultimately leading to my personal vision, mission, and values. You learn so much about you and where you can improve, naturally leading to your improved positive take on things.

To all the women reading this, I encourage you to embark on your own journey of self-discovery. Define your vision, mission, and values. Establish your deal breakers. Be sure to revisit them yearly as they are not set in stone. We are always growing. Maintain a current personal blueprint that reflects your true self and guides you towards a fulfilling and purposeful life. Remember, you are the architect of your destiny. Build it with intention and unwavering belief in your worth and potential.

There is resilience and strength that lie within each of us. It's a reminder that even in our darkest moments, we have the power to redefine our path and emerge stronger. By aligning our lives with our deepest values and aspirations, we can navigate any storm and find our way to brighter, more fulfilling days. You are more than you are today. You are a constantly growing powerhouse of greatness. Let your personal blueprint be your guiding light, illuminating your journey toward an ever-expanding life of purpose, joy, and connection. And remember, like a disco ball, you can bring light and sparkle to every situation, making the ordinary extraordinary.

Favorite Quote

Let all that you do be done in love. 1 Corinthians 16:14

Recommended Affirmation

-Business affirmation-

Do the right thing and you can't go wrong.

Jenny's Special Offer

Dive deeper into Jenny DeBolt's inspiring story by visiting uscleaning.com/sixfigurechicks to download a complimentary copy of her chapter in *Six-Figure Chicks, Phoenix*. Plus, don't miss the chance to get your own copy of the full *Six-Figure Chicks, Phoenix* book, filled with empowering stories of women who have turned their challenges into success.

About Jenny DeBolt,

Owner Us Cleaning Solutions LLC

Jenny DeBolt, founder of Us Cleaning Solutions, merges business success with social impact. Her 7-figure cleaning business and book "Suicide & Sequins" highlight her dedication to suicide prevention and grief support. Guided by spiritual values and compassion, Jenny's work balances impressive business achievements with a heartfelt commitment to others, creating a legacy that extends beyond profits. Her life integrates joy, gratitude, and service, making a profound societal impact.

Kimberly Mitchell's *Story*

At twenty-three years old, I made a big decision that changed the trajectory of my life. I decided to drive to Los Cabos, Mexico with a girl I had met only six months prior, intending to stay for a year. Fourteen years and two months later I returned to the U.S., with a husband, two kids and a wealth of experience.

I have always been outgoing, eager to travel and open-minded about what I may learn along the way. The first year and a half in Cabo was fun meeting new people, but it was hard to get my footing and navigate living in a different country. I tell my daughters, "Right now, everything looks nice, we have a nice business, a nice house. But then, in the beginning, I just had a mattress on the floor and a trash bag for my dirty clothes. It was not bougie by any stretch of the imagination." The main lesson I learned from that first experience in Mexico was not to give up.

Getting a job in Mexico was tricky. As an American, speaking English had to be the main reason for getting a particular job–in vacation clubs, timeshares, or real estate–where they need English spoken to foreigners. With limitations on what I could do workwise, I started with commission-based sales at a resort in Cabo. Then I got a job as a verification loan officer in Puerto Vallarta. I had worked with my dad in his mortgage business and as an office manager for the owner of multiple used car lots, so I knew the terminology and basics of financing.

I met my husband, Wes, through work, and when he got promoted, we moved back to Cabo. I had my daughter, Samantha, in 2006. Then after four years in Cabo, we returned to Vallarta where I had my second daughter, Sophia, in 2011.

Just a couple years into my time in Mexico, when I had just turned twenty-five, my great-grandmother died at 103 years old. We had been very close. She raised my dad more than his own mom did. For the final six months of her life, she was in a large nursing home that appeared to me to be more of a human warehouse than a care home. It was hard to see her in that environment, and it made an impact on me. Little did I know a seed had been planted for my future business.

At that point, all four of my grandparents were still alive. I could see them aging when I would return to the U.S. for visits and was acutely aware of the challenges they had to deal with. My dad's dad got Parkinson's, and that was my first experience of hospice care. Then we moved my dad's mom into a group home. Though we experienced a lot of home care situations with my grandparents, we didn't realize until much later (two years before we moved) that the baby boomers needed home care.

After moving back to the states, we began a process with a franchise organization. Our business is not a franchise; however, we found the franchise process valuable because it helped us choose and operate our business more soundly. They identified our strengths and weaknesses and what an ideal business for us would be. What I walked away with was the non-medical home care concept.

It was an opportunity to make things better for seniors than what my grandparents went through. There were a lot of businesses for sale that we looked at, but having young kids, we knew we wouldn't buy any restaurants, clubs or bakeries. When the home care business was put in front of us, it just made sense. They only had fifteen caregivers and eleven clients when we purchased it for $300k. Now we have 200 employees, over 170 clients and last year, our business was worth $3M.

As a family-owned business, I own 55 percent, and my husband owns 45 percent. We have caregivers who go to the homes and do the caregiving, but we manage everything else. Wes does sales and talks with clients, and I manage business operations day in and day out. In the beginning, I also did all the accounting, bookkeeping, taxes, insurance, etc. After our first year in business, we doubled in size and had to get help in the office. We hired part time first, then full-time office employees. Year after year we grew and scaled. Now I have eight full time employees in the office and two marketing staff members.

An important lesson I learned along the way in business was to not be so afraid. It's important to have faith that what you're doing will work. We jumped with both feet into an industry we'd never been in. At the time of buying the business, it was scary. But every time I felt scared, we just figured out the next step. I joined a local association for the industry and got involved in women's networking. It's vital to surround yourself with like-minded women who are growing. Each decade, particularly as women, we care less and less about what other people think. This is a superpower. If I had that beginning phase to do over again, I would tell myself to just do what feels right and good, and don't lose sleep over tough decisions.

At 48, I value my health and well-being immensely. I do boxing classes, spin classes with weights, and barre classes. I get up at 5 a.m. every morning to meditate, journal and exercise to boost my energy. I have longevity on both sides of my family. My grandparents lived well into their eighties and nineties. My husband's mom just turned ninety-five.

I believe in living today like it's going to be your last but also living like you're going to be 100. I have several clients in their nineties, and I ask my teenage daughters, "What kind of ninety-year-old do you want to be?" I have clients who have lost their vision and/or hearing but are moving and happy. And I have clients who are twenty-five years younger than them but are angry, bitter, in pain and unhappy. The choice is up to us.

My parents live joyfully and have always been my biggest supporters. When I told them I was moving to Mexico, they were a little freaked out but encouraged me. My dad said, "I knew when you were two at the beach in California, that was your happy place." When we moved back to Phoenix, it was a huge help having our village of family here to help us with the girls during our first year of the business. Since my dad retired thirteen years ago, every school year he puts the half days on his calendar and picks up my daughters from school to spend time with them. Having that quality time with family is the main reason we moved back to Phoenix. Once my parents are gone though, I plan to live at the beach again.

It is no surprise with my love for travel that I moved to another country at such a young age. Or that I married a man from another country (Wes is from Saskatchewan, Canada). It is my goal to see all fifty states (I have seen twenty-six), and I've visited Greece, Italy, France, Ireland, South Africa, Zimbabwe, Argentina, and Panama. I recently went with my family to Kenya and Tanzania. In Mexico, Wes and I were always known as "the Mitchell B&B" because we had a revolving door for friends and family to visit us.

I wish more people traveled and were more open-minded. I believe the world would be a better place overall if they did. People would be kinder to one another. One of my top values, kindness, is a big motivator for our business, Home With Help. I believe in treating people with equal kindness; the CEO is the same as the janitor.

Overall, the village you surround yourself with, be it blood or chosen, determines who you support and who supports you. That's why I serve on the board of NAWBO (National Association of Women Business Owners). They're big on advocacy and were pivotal in getting a significant bill passed on October 25th, 1988, stating that women didn't have to have a man sign for a business loan.

I've also donated to Women for Women International, and I participate in KNOW and The Foundress locally. In all of these organizations, I love the networking component, supporting women, referring business and learning. Women helping women goes a long way in making the world a better place, especially when we can bring more women into higher positions. The only way to get them there is this: as soon as one of us gets a seat, we must give another woman a seat next to us. Then we can travel upwards together.

Favorite Quote

"Travel is fatal to prejudice, bigotry, and narrow-mindedness, and many of our people need it sorely on these accounts. Broad, wholesome, charitable views of men and things cannot be acquired by vegetating in one little corner of the earth all one's lifetime."

— MARK T

Recommended Affirmation

I write in my journal every day starting with,
"Today is going to be a beautiful day!"

Kimberly's Special Offer

In her chapter, Kimberly Mitchell shares her journey of strength and compassion. To support you further, Kimberly is offering a special resource for those impacted by Alzheimer's Disease. Visit homewithhelp.net/women-and-alzheimers-disease/ to explore invaluable insights and receive guidance tailored for women navigating this challenging journey.

About Kimberly Mitchell,

President Home With Help

Kimberly Mitchell is a dedicated mother, wife, and co-owner of Home With Help, an organization that provides non-medical companionship, homemaking, and personal care services in Arizona. After building a family and life in Mexico for 14 years, she moved back home to Phoenix to advocate for the elderly. Passionate about supporting women, she is on the board of NAWBO and involved in Women for Women International, KNOW and The Foundress.

Kimberly Mylls' *Story*

Earning a six-figure income is a lot like finding the love of your life. You go on a series of dates, each one teaching you something new about what you want, and more importantly, what you don't want. If you could take the best traits from each of those dates and combine them, you'd have the perfect partner. The same principle applies to building a six-figure career. Each job, boss, and relationship bring a lesson, shaping your path until you find your strengths and passion and turn them into the perfect career.

My journey to a six-figure income didn't follow a straight line, but rather a winding road filled with valuable detours. I started in the corporate world, where I had a job in the publishing industry. I loved it until I started to see the industry changing, and I was tired of working long hours building someone else's empire. I had the income many dream of, but something was missing. Despite the prestige and financial security, my corporate role lacked the passion and purpose I craved. I had accomplished all I wanted in the industry and had no idea what to do next.

I realized that to find true fulfillment, I needed to take a leap of faith and walk away from what no longer served me. It was a terrifying decision but also an exciting one. I transitioned into something completely new–network marketing. This was my catalyst, the jumpstart I needed to become a serial entrepreneur.

Leaving corporate America was like ending a long-term relationship. It was comfortable and familiar, but it wasn't my soulmate. Network marketing was like a whirlwind romance, exciting and full of potential. Through this venture, I discovered a new passion for coaching, teaching, and training. I loved showing others how to succeed and realized this was a cornerstone of my future career.

The beauty of network marketing was its flexibility and the community it fostered. I thrived on the personal connections and the chance to mentor others. It wasn't just about the products or the business model; it was about empowering people to achieve their goals and showing them how to build a business for themselves. This experience laid the foundation for my future endeavors.

During that time, I was in an environment which encouraged personal development–something I didn't think I needed until I understood the power of manifestation. Personal development became a staple of my success. It gave me the confidence to take risks and dream bigger. The tangible part was that I was able to retire my husband from a corporate job he hated, and together we opened a specialized gym.

Owning a brick-and-mortar business was a whole new ballgame for me. We made loads of mistakes and realized everyone was getting paid except for us! Something had to change. We listened to our community and realized there was one thing all the parents wanted. It was exercise for their children. So, my husband and I pivoted–we sold the gym and created a kids' summer program and after-school activities. 15 years later it was one of the best business decisions we have made.

This pivot was a revelation. Without the experience of running the gym, we wouldn't have built a thriving mountain bike summer camp.

It was another piece of the puzzle, bringing me closer to my ideal career. Each step, whether it seemed successful or not, contributed to my growth and understanding of what I truly wanted to do.

One constant through all these ventures was my love for building businesses and teaching and training others how to grow and scale. I loved pieces of everything I did, but what got me the most fired up was teaching others how to succeed.

I realized that many women had big dreams and business ideas but didn't know how to start them and how to make them profitable. I created a mastermind just for them so they could have all the tools needed to launch a successful business. What I learned was that ambitious, high achieving women want to be in a room of like-minded and like-hearted women. I heard the feedback and created a collective for women earning seven figures.

It was exciting showing women how to grow businesses. I saw women light up with passion and excitement, but one thing became abundantly clear. No matter how great the product or service someone has, if you don't know how to "sell" it, it simply won't matter. This is why I built a sales training and consulting business, where I could focus entirely on building sales confidence.

Through all these experiences, I learned three key lessons:

1. First, never be afraid to walk away when something isn't serving you anymore. My motto has always been: "say no to the good, so you can say yes to the great." It's easy to stay in a comfortable but unfulfilling situation out of fear or habit. But true growth happens when you step out of your comfort zone and pursue what truly excites you.
2. Second, every experience, whether it seems like a success or failure, is valuable. Each job, boss, and relationship teaches you something. Collect the best lessons and apply them to

your next venture. It's like dating; each relationship brings you closer to understanding what you truly want and need.

3. Finally, always be open to feedback and be willing to change directions. Flexibility and adaptability are crucial in creating a fulfilling career. Sometimes, closing one door is the only way to open another.

Now I look back at my journey and see how each step was essential in creating my perfect career. It's like crafting the perfect partner from all the best qualities of your past relationships. My path wasn't linear, but it was filled with invaluable lessons and experiences that shaped who I am today.

So, take that leap of faith. Walk away from what no longer serves you and embrace the unknown. Gather lessons from every experience and let them guide you. Be open to feedback and willing to pivot when necessary. And most importantly, believe in yourself and your ability to create a career that brings both financial success and personal fulfillment.

In my own journey, I went from a high-paying corporate job to network marketing, opened a gym, wrote a book, started children's programs, and created a business incubator. All those experiences led me to today, founder of MI7, a millionaire collective, and founder of Sales Spark, a sales training and consulting business. I took the things I loved from each career move, focused on my superpowers and designed a business that matched exactly what I wanted.

When it comes to love, we can't always create the perfect person (until the movie *Weird Science* becomes a reality). But, when it comes to your career, you absolutely can!

Favorite Quote

"Go confidently in the direction of your dreams! Live the life you've imagined. As you simplify your life, the laws of the universe will be simpler."

— HENRY DAVID THOREAU

Recommended Affirmation

I am grateful for all I have and all the opportunities coming my way today

Kimberly's Special Offer

As a serial entrepreneur what I have learned is the key to success is sales confidence. You can offer the best service or the best product but if you don't know how to sell, your business will be a constant uphill battle. Master sales and you can achieve anything

www.salesspark.biz

About Kimberly Mylls,

Owner, Sales Spark

Kimberly Mylls is a serial entrepreneur and co-owner of Sales Spark, a sales consultancy agency. She co-founded MI7, a mastermind group for seven-figure women entrepreneurs, and Kids Dojo, a nonprofit empowering youth. Kimberly co-authored "Boys Before Business" and has built multiple six-figure businesses. Passionate about mentoring, she empowers women to start and grow successful businesses, proving that dreams can become reality.

Lisa Riley's *Story*

Have you ever wondered how some people seem to have all the luck in the world? How do they always find themselves in the right place at the right time, and get to do amazing things? Well, I'm here to tell you that luck is not just a matter of chance. It's also a matter of choice. It's about being prepared, flexible, and willing to take risks. It's about saying yes to the right opportunities and no to the wrong ones. It's about making the best decision you can with the information and time you have, and trusting yourself.

I'm going to share with you some of the times I said yes to opportunities: how I went from being an average clarinet player in high school to becoming an all-state bass clarinetist, how being in the right place led to graduate education, how networking and mentoring opened doors for me that I didn't even know existed, and how I switched careers and became a successful business broker and lower middle market advisor. I hope that my story will inspire you to say yes to the right opportunities and to be open to new challenges and experiences.

I was just one of the many clarinet players in my high school band, and I knew I would never stand out or excel. I was okay, but not great. One day, our band director announced that we needed someone to play the bass clarinet, which is a bigger and deeper-sounding instrument that not many people played. It looked intimidating but also intriguing. I decided to give it a try. It was a smart move, because I discovered that although there were hundreds of clarinet players, there were few who played the bass clarinet. I practiced hard, learned new skills, and improved my musical abilities. I became an all-state bass clarinetist, which meant that I got to play with the best musicians in the state. It was a wonderful experience and a confidence booster. I learned that sometimes, you have to find your niche and do something different to get noticed and succeed.

I was always a good student and loved learning. My siblings and I are first generation college students, although my parents had always emphasized education. During my senior year of college, I was sprawled out in old, ragged sweats working late afternoon on a paper in the Department. One of my professor's Notre Dame co-authors on a national study saw me and asked my professor about me. He told him who I was and made an introduction. At that moment, I decided I was going to apply to grad school to get my master's degree. However, my father had some significant health issues, so I decided not to apply that year. Unbeknownst to me, my professor and others had written letters of recommendation and sent them in. During this time, I worked at a temporary staffing company. I did everything from cleaning toilets to architectural blueprints to administrative assistant at a college. I was offered several jobs; however, I was focused. A year later when I applied, they still had all the letters of recommendation in a file.

During grad school, I delayed vacations, ate ramen noodles for months on end, took a job waiting tables at a nightclub in order to keep paying bills and focused on this amazing opportunity. I learned a lot from the professors and the classmates there. I was hired as a Research Assistant and was fortunate to co-author several papers.

I finished my master's degree and decided to earn a doctoral degree so I could continue as a Research Assistant. One week prior to the start of the following semester, I was asked to teach an upper-level family course at Notre Dame. They needed someone to fill in as the professor had left the university. I was nervous and unsure, but I said yes. I had never taught before, but I was willing to try. The textbook had been ordered, and the syllabus had been shared with students. I had to come up with homework assignments that were already laid out, prepare each class and stay ahead of the students.

The first day, my legs were shaking so badly that I was glad I had decided to sit behind the desk and had the students in a semi-circle. It turned out to be one of the best classes I ever taught. The students were engaged and interested. They gave me positive feedback and said that they learned a lot. I also learned a lot from them and from the experience of teaching. It was a challenging but rewarding experience. I learned how to communicate effectively, engage the students, and manage the classroom. I also had to balance my teaching duties with my research work.

I spent the next year working on my dissertation. I also did 'practice' interviews to prepare for the job market. I sent out my vitae to some open college positions to see if they would be a fit. I got some nos and some yeses–leading to in-person interviews! I also applied for some research positions at research organizations, and had several long phone call interviews, however, I did not move forward to the next step. It was spring, and I decided to simply focus on finishing my dissertation.

Then something unexpected happened. My advisor received a call from his alma mater, a university in another state. They asked him if one of his recent PhD graduates had already taken a position. She had. He then asked them why they were not considering me. They said that I didn't apply. He told them that I was a great candidate, that they should consider me and that they'd have my application within twenty-four hours. He then told me to apply. I did, and I got invited for two and a half days of full interviews. I went there and met with the faculty, the students, and the administrators. It was a very intense two and a half days, from breakfasts to late evening dinners. Although it was truly a "who you know" that opened the door, I had to perform better than most. They wanted someone who already had their doctorate, and I was still a year out. Prior to leaving on my flight, they offered me a position and I said yes. In part because I would be less than two hours from my parents, siblings and extended family. I was excited. However, there was no written contract yet. They said that they would send it to me soon.

A week later, I received a call from one of the research organizations offering me a job. I was stunned. The research position was my dream job, and I had almost given up hope of getting it. I felt a surge of emotions. I knew this research position was a once-in-a-lifetime opportunity. It aligned with my interests and goals, and it offered more prestige and salary. However, I told them that I appreciated their offer, but I had to decline. I explained that I had already committed to another job and I didn't feel right about changing my mind. They said they were disappointed, but they respected my decision.

I moved to a new state and started my job as a college professor. I taught courses and did research for federal and local government and organizations. I enjoyed my work and my colleagues. I earned tenure and promotion. I also met my future husband.

We moved to Arizona as my husband received a great opportunity, and we built a house. I decided to take the plunge and say yes to a new opportunity.

So, I joined a business brokerage firm where I could use my skills and knowledge to help business owners sell their businesses and buyers find the right business for them!

As a brand new (one month) broker, I attended my first International Business Brokers Association (IBBA) conference. During this conference, I was a sponge and learned so much. We help clients evaluate their businesses, market them, negotiate with buyers, and successfully exit. Additionally, we assist buyers in finding the right businesses, due diligence, securing financing, and successfully buying. It's a lot of work and a lot of responsibility, but it is so rewarding and satisfying.

After my first IBBA Conference, I was asked to join a committee and be part of the team to start a quarterly survey. I accepted and have continued to work on that survey since 2011.

Three years into my new career, my father passed away. This life altering event made me think about what I wanted to do. I decided to start my own company, with a true focus on clients.

As a boutique firm, we love helping people achieve their goals and dreams. I never know what each day will bring. I'm blessed as I get to meet many interesting people and help them with their transitions. I've also made great friends and mentors in the industry. I became an expert in valuing, marketing, and selling businesses. I also like the challenge and variety of working with different types of businesses and industries while keeping up with changing trends. Holding my first $200k check was thrilling.

This led me to saying yes to board positions on our local association and the IBBA, eventually becoming the chair of both organizations. When I received a call asking me to be chair of such a large organization, I have to admit I was honored, awed, and flabbergasted. I prayed, talked with my husband, and decided to say yes. I have never regretted that decision and oh, did I continue to grow.

Saying yes to the right opportunities leads to success. I've shared how I became an all-state bass clarinetist, a college professor, and a business broker by being prepared, flexible, and adventurous. I have said yes to unexpected opportunities and stepped out of my comfort zone, changing and evolving on my journey in life. I have also shared some of the lessons and insights that I learned along the way. I hope that my story has inspired you to say yes to the right opportunities and to be open to new challenges and experiences. You never know where they might lead you and what you might achieve. Remember, luck is being in the right place at the right time, but it's also being prepared, flexible, and adventurous.

Favorite Quote

The Serenity Prayer:
"God, grant me the serenity to accept the things I cannot change, the courage to change the things I can, and the wisdom to know the difference"

Recommended Affirmation

Today, I Live, Laugh and Love!

Lisa's Special Offer

Unlock the potential of your business with a free and confidential consultation from Delta Business Advisors. Whether you're planning to sell, merge, or grow, their expert team offers personalized guidance to help you achieve your goals. Start your journey towards a successful business transition with trusted advisors who understand your unique needs. Visit deltabusinessadvisors.com to schedule your consultation today.

About Lisa Riley,

CEO & Founder Delta Business Advisors

Lisa is the CEO and Founder of Delta Business Advisors, LLC, a boutique business brokerage and lower M&A advisory firm. She is the recipient of numerous prestigious awards, an educator and a can-do entrepreneur. She has served on industry Association boards and been elected as Chair. When not working or learning, Lisa loves to enjoy her time off with her spouse, traveling and spending time with friends.

Lucy Kairalla's *Story*

Do you know that old saying, *"The more you work, the more money you make?"* It used to be my motto. Well, I learned that this motto wasn't as wise as it sounded. After I worked my life away, I decided I needed a different motto: "*Make money, have fun, help people*." Yes... I still want to make money.

It all started at the age of nineteen. I was finishing my college degree in Sao Paulo, Brazil and working (a lot) for a man in the political arena. On an errand to get signatures, I visited a modern marketing agency with a great vibe. While there, I encountered two impressive women who were clearly business partners. They exuded confidence, professionalism, and pure joy. I remember vividly what these two women looked like, what they were wearing–dressed in black–and how they carried themselves. After spending time with those two women and watching them that entire afternoon, I knew I wanted to become a business owner like them.

I became a marketing manager at a very young age, working for the Convention & Visitors Association for the fifth largest city in the world, Sao Paulo. My goal was to be the best in a place where everyone around me was also "the best." Speaking perfect English was going to give me that edge. So, in 2005 I moved to the States and promised myself that I would only stop learning English once I started dreaming in English. I was studying hard to get an MBA, working hard, and on my way to accomplishing my goal. But after experiencing life in the US, I didn't want to go back to Brazil.

I couldn't wait to show corporate America what I was made of. My first real job in the U.S. was as a Sales Executive for a healthcare company. I had to meet a quota of fifteen in-person meetings a week with health insurance brokers. It seemed impossible at that time. In order to find these brokers, I became a member of Women in Financial Services (WIFS). I was amazed that business deals were being made in every corner of the room; the power of women coming together and helping each other grow their businesses was real. I got more involved and met my quota with ease. This experience showed me the power of community, connection, and women supporting each other.

The image of the two women I had seen in Brazil, leading their business confidently and successfully became even stronger to me. Determined to follow in their footsteps, I contemplated opening a marketing agency. Everyone in my family was an employee, and I didn't have a role model to follow who was a business owner. However, I knew this one thing... I wasn't going to be an employee in the long run. I knew if I was ever going to work for a corporation again, it would be my own.

The pivotal moment was a conversation with a client and business owner, Joel Slenning. I asked him if he thought I could own a business. He replied, "Yes," with conviction. Then I asked, "What if I fail?" and he said, "If you don't try, you've already failed." His confidence in me was empowering. His words especially made an impact because I'd done a thorough analysis of his business and his competition a few years back, and I gave him a marketing plan—which he implemented—and his business grew exponentially. I knew Joel was the right person to talk to, and in 2015, I got a partner (remember - two women in black) and Plain Language Marketing, LLC was born.

My journey in marketing and my commitment to clear and effective English communication became the foundation of my business. If you study the science of marketing, you quickly understand the importance of the words on the page, the visuals, and the channels of distribution.

Marketing is like asking someone out on a date.

Branding is the reason they say yes.

I always tell my clients, “Your branding and marketing need each other,” and that perfect synergy of the two is exactly what we do at Plain Language Marketing – www.PlainLanguageMatters.com. Today, we are a team of nine people, but things didn’t start out so easily.

When we first started, we worked really hard and only made $800 in that first year. We sold one single logo. The client loved it so much that she teared up. And that was when I realized that the satisfaction of seeing the client happy was much more valuable than the money. It was a sign that I was on the right path. After three years, we reached half a million in revenue. This growth was fueled by the small victories that kept us motivated and focused.

The path to owning a business is hard but can be rewarding. It’s easy to get discouraged by comparing where you are today to where you want to be in the future. But if you look at where you started compared to where you are now, it’s a much more powerful motivator.

During the course of my journey, I became a wife, a student, a mother, a dog mom, and a business owner. Women often juggle many roles, and it can be a lot of pressure. Through challenges I faced, like divorce and an early failed business partnership, I learned two important lessons:

1. It's okay not to be perfect as long as you're acting with your heart.

2. You don't have to go it alone.

My successes were never just mine; there were always people advising, supporting, and helping me along the way. When I'm feeling overwhelmed, I remind myself of the people who are priorities in my life.

There were many times when I was too busy prioritizing my business. I missed important moments with my children and husband at that time. Today I prioritize a balanced life. I never miss a volleyball competition for my kids because it keeps my energy high. I can be a better advisor for my clients and a better leader for my team if my energy is high.

As I look back on my journey, it becomes clear why my motto had to evolve. The old saying, *"The more you work, the more money you make,"* served me well in the early days, pushing me to achieve academic excellence, career milestones, and eventually, my dream of owning a business. However, through the years, I realized that relentless hard work without balance was not sustainable. The encounters with inspiring women, the power of community, and the joy of helping others led me to see life through a different lens.

Witnessing the positive impact my work had on clients and experiencing the fulfillment of being present for my family, I understood that success is multifaceted. My new motto, *"Make money, have fun, help people,"* encapsulates this broader perspective. It acknowledges my ambition, but it also emphasizes the importance of joy and contribution. This change reflects a deeper understanding that true success is not just about financial gain, but also about enjoying the journey and making a positive difference in the lives of others.

Favorite Quote

"Clear is better than Clever"

— LUCY KAIRALLA

Recommended Affirmation

Vision without strategy is an illusion. Go for your dreams.

Lucy's Special Offer

Unlock the potential of your online presence! As a special gift to our readers, you are invited to receive a complimentary 16-point website and SEO audit. This is your chance to gain expert insights and elevate your digital strategy. Schedule your free audit today by visiting www.plainlanguagematters.com/contact/.

About Lucy Kairalla,

Founder & Marketing Strategist

Lucy Kairalla is the CEO and chief marketing strategist at Plain Language Marketing. She's earned two MBA degrees and is a certified SEO SEMrush specialist. She serves businesses ready to scale and has mentored and supported hundreds of women entrepreneurs. With over 15 years of experience, Lucy is an expert in helping complex businesses communicate clearly with their customers. Her agency uses groundbreaking organic marketing and Ai tools supporting every stage of business.

Monica May-Dunn's *Story*

Do you know a twenty-two-year-old female working in a male-dominated industry? Well, I do. This is MY story.

As a young professional woman, I often faced significant challenges as I strived for validation and recognition. It took me over thirty years to understand the value of being seen and heard as a woman in business. Proving my competence and expertise meant navigating a landscape where my presence and opinions were undervalued or overlooked. Achieving visibility and being heard required resilience, confidence, and a supportive network. Facing these challenges has been instrumental in shaping my professional journey and getting me to where I am today.

Those challenges not only tested my limits but also expanded them, contributing to my success and shaping me into a more capable and determined professional. I began as an assistant controller in 1990, then became the controller, then CFO. After many years, I was promoted to Vice President, and after decades in the business, the founder and my mentor, Donald Graham, asked if I was interested in acquiring the company one day. In 2015, my immediate response was, "Yes, absolutely." Then in 2020, the world faced an unexpected health pandemic that changed the landscape of doing business, especially in Arizona.

Our entire escrow department went to another title company in March of 2020 right before everyone had to mandatorily close for Covid. Our founder's first employee of forty years and her escrow staff went with them. It was a very stressful time for everyone, including the owner. During this time, he was ready to give up and shut down the company for good. I reassured him that the company still had value and reminded him that we still had open escrows.

I had an epiphany when I saw that Annette Anderson (Escrow Officer since the 90's) was having to close her restaurant temporarily for Covid. We had remained friends over the years, so I decided to give her a call. I asked her, "Are you needing something to do?" I told her I needed help. Culture, core values, and a code of ethics—we were ready! Annette rejoined the company, and together, with Olivia Limon and myself, we worked diligently on training the staff, hiring new employees, and creating a new brand for our company. My vision was to become bigger and better than ever before, and that is exactly what we did.

Even when the pandemic severely impacted local small businesses, I managed to maintain our business through PPP funding. Having a small staff has been key in maintaining and growing our business. We gained momentum and established record-breaking years that followed. The close-knit nature of our team fosters strong collaboration and agility, enabling us to adapt quickly to changing market conditions and seize new opportunities. Each team member's contributions are highly valued, and their diverse skills and dedication have driven our success.

So here I was once again, navigating setbacks and overcoming adversity. With the business sale still pending in August of 2020, I wasn't sure if I should take the risk and purchase the company. But then I remembered that Don trusted me. I had to trust myself. Despite my reservations, I gained the confidence to tackle complex problems and made the right decision. By 2023, I became the sole owner of the company I had dedicated so much time and energy to.

As the owner of the company where I started when I was only twenty-two years old, I learned some very valuable lessons. Each obstacle presented an opportunity to gain experience and grow, teaching me invaluable lessons about resilience, adaptability, and perseverance. More importantly, it presented me with an opportunity that one can only dream of. Arizona Escrow & Financial Corp. is now one of the valley's top independently woman-owned escrow companies in Arizona.

Our rebranding over the past two years has been equally important. We brought back former clients who realized we were still going strong, even after the pandemic. One of the biggest lessons I learned was the importance of listening to people. Our cohesive and dynamic work environment has not only preserved the integrity of our business but also propelled us to new heights, demonstrating that a committed and capable small team can achieve remarkable results.

Just when I thought I had positioned myself as a leading woman in business, something happened that made me feel like the twenty-two-year-old female in the room again. I had a scheduled meeting with a gentleman in the industry. After canceling the first meeting, we set up a second one, and as I waited patiently, he was late again. He had to make it known that he was dropping off his Porsche to get it worked on. Though I was taken aback by his unprofessionalism, nothing prepared me for what he said next: "Well, if you would have told me you were the owner I would have taken you more seriously." Completely stunned, I thought to myself, this was not okay. It forever changed me as a woman business owner. I re-dedicated myself to providing servant leadership and ensuring that everyone felt respected, appreciated, supported, and heard.

Moving forward, I have every intention of growing the company through the principles I have believed in since my early career. Our beautiful new office is in Central Phoenix, and within the next few years, I hope to open more branches in the East and far West Valley. We are focused on building our new brand and working with more professionals in the valley. Over the past two years, we hired social media marketing agencies to help create brand awareness and highlight the many services we provide. Years ago, there wasn't much competition, but in this competitive industry, we are investing in ourselves so people can learn more about us and how we can provide value to those needing escrow services. We also encourage our employees to be more active on social media and share their experiences.

Last year, with the support and confidence of my team, I started a new podcast called Practical and Positive Leadership. My podcast allows me to bring on special guests and authors, mostly women business owners, to share their experiences in leadership, best practices, and other valuable insights to inspire and empower other women. I just finished my tenth podcast episode, and the full playlist and episodes can be found on our company website. You can listen on mainstream platforms like Amazon-Audible Music, iTunes, and Spotify.

I also wanted to be more involved with the community. I joined local networking groups and chambers to connect with other business owners. I am involved with CREW (Commercial Real Estate Women), the Women in Commercial Real Estate Network, WATT (Women at The Top), Vistage, WPO, and Provisors. I was featured on the cover of AZRE Magazine and contributed to the CREW feature. I am thrilled to share that I was recently named one of the Most Influential Women in Commercial Real Estate by AZRE Magazine in their July 2024 issue.

Earlier this year, I was also featured in THRIVE! – Behind Every Woman, with the Women in CRE network.

It's been beautiful to see the generational growth and success of the women in business in my family – from my mother to me to my daughter. My mother, a successful business owner herself, has been one of the most influential figures in my life. Her unwavering dedication, entrepreneurial spirit, and resilience have been a constant source of inspiration. Her independence and progress were extraordinary for her time. She started her first job when I turned five years old and learned how to drive for the first time. She is still one of my biggest fans and even helped our company administration during the pandemic.

My family have been my champions through all of this. Their consistent support has allowed me to commute from living in Yuma to staying two to three nights per week in Phoenix. I have done this for twenty-four years, and thanks to my husband's support, I am still able to travel back and forth every week. My daughter and her family live in Yuma as well. In fact, we all live on the same property, so we are very close to each other. I have gained much inspiration from my daughter too. Her success and achievements as a young Director of Planning and Neighborhood Services for The City of Yuma brings me such joy as a mother. There is such power in women inspiring each other in business, especially within a family.

If there is one thing I can share with my grandchildren, I will tell them not to be afraid and to face their fears. I will show them that every obstacle is an opportunity for growth. I will encourage them to use every learning experience as a stepping stone to build confidence and resilience. I will emphasize the importance of perseverance, believing in themselves, and understanding that failures are just lessons in disguise.

Favorite Quote

"We need women at all levels, including the top, to change the dynamic, reshape the conversation, to make sure women's voices are heard and heeded, not overlooked and ignored."

— SHERYL SANDBERG

Recommended Affirmation

I have experienced challenges in the past,
and I am more resilient because of this

Monica's Special Offer

As a special thank you for diving into my journey, I invite you to join me on the *Practical and Positive Leadership Podcast*. Tune in for insightful conversations and leadership tips designed to empower and inspire you. Your next step to practical leadership awaits—listen in here: www.arizonaescrow.com/practical-positive-leadership-podcast/ and continue your path to greatness!

About Monica May-Dunn,

CEO/CFO Arizona Escrow & Financial

Monica's expertise and leadership have been instrumental in propelling AEF to the forefront of the escrow and financial services industry. She began her journey with the company in 1990 as the assistant to the Controller and swiftly advanced to the role of Controller by 1992. Recognizing her exceptional skills and dedication, Monica was appointed as VP/CFO in 2000, further solidifying her pivotal role within the organization. Her career continued to ascend as she became Vice President in 2010. In 2023, Monica's commitment and vision culminated in her becoming the 100% owner of AEF, marking a significant milestone in both her career and the company's history. Monica was honored as one of the Most Influential Women in 2024.

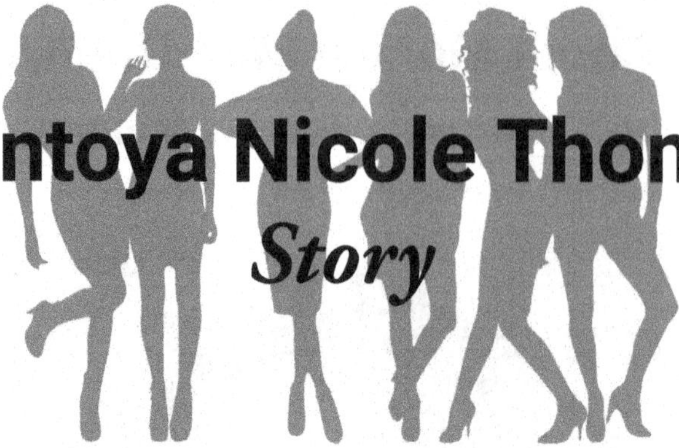

Shantoya Nicole Thomas' *Story*

Success stories often seem like overnight miracles, but those of us who have lived them know that they are the result of countless hours of dedication, perseverance, and sometimes sheer stubbornness. My journey to earning a six-figure income is no different. It's a tale of grit, growth, and a relentless pursuit of a dream that, at times, felt impossible. But if I can do it, so can you. Here's how I got here.

I grew up in Phoenix, AZ where opportunities were limited, and dreams of making it big often seemed like fairy tales. My parents worked hard and hustled harder to make ends meet, and they instilled in me a strong work ethic. However, they also inadvertently passed on a scarcity mindset. We moved often–California, Oregon, Washington–searching for a better life, but always ending up back home in Phoenix. Success, in their eyes, was reserved for a lucky few, and it certainly didn't seem like it was meant for someone like me.

Despite this, I was always a dreamer. I envisioned a life of abundance, where financial stress didn't dictate every decision. I wanted to travel, explore, and live life on my own terms. But the path to that life was unclear. I didn't have a roadmap, and more importantly, I didn't have any role models who had achieved what I wanted.

During college, I started providing childcare to make ends meet. I had no idea what I was doing in college, but my Mom always said to go into healthcare or be a secretary for job security. I entered the corporate world, ready to climb the ladder of success. I took on every project, worked late hours, and sacrificed weekends, all in the name of proving myself. My hard work did pay off, to an extent. I received promotions and pay raises, but the financial reward never seemed to match the effort I was putting in. I was constantly exhausted and felt like I was on a hamster wheel, running endlessly but getting nowhere.

This period was a significant learning curve for me. I realized that hard work alone wasn't the answer. I needed to work smarter, not just harder. But I didn't have the luxury of quitting my job to figure out how. I had bills to pay and responsibilities to manage. It started to seem that my side hustle, childcare, could be more rewarding than the corporate slow climb. But how?

The turning point came when I decided to invest in myself. I began reading books on personal development, finance, and entrepreneurship. I attended seminars and workshops, and I sought out mentors who had achieved the success I was striving for. One of the most impactful pieces of advice I received was to invest in myself, both in terms of education and personal growth. A huge turning point in my life was the realization that I had to work on myself first. This involved long walks and talks with God. I needed to know my purpose. This led to a joyous season in the fitness industry. I learned to love working on me, and in return, others genuinely embraced me.

I learned the importance of setting boundaries and managing my time effectively. I discovered the power of saying "no" to tasks and projects that didn't align with my goals. More importantly, I realized that I needed to shift my mindset from one of scarcity to one of abundance. This mental shift is crucial. It allowed me to see opportunities where I had previously seen obstacles.

With newfound knowledge and a renewed sense of purpose, I began to explore side hustles that aligned with my passions and skills. I started advertising my childcare services as a business. Although I didn't have all the business savvy, yet I started learning. One thing I knew was that I enjoyed caring for others. This was the beginning of building my professional and personal brand.

Through this season, I connected with a community of like-minded individuals, many of whom were also striving to achieve financial independence. This network became an invaluable resource. We shared ideas, supported each other, and collaborated on projects. I realized the power of community and collaboration in achieving success.

One of the key lessons I learned from my mentors was the importance of creating multiple income streams. I began exploring other avenues to generate income. I launched a boutique business with the crafts we'd do at the childcare. The crafting boutique was a joy, and it provided passive income while doing something I was already doing in an environment that I loved.

I also started consulting, leveraging my experience to help others in childcare homes. This side hustle not only increased my income but also expanded my professional network. The more I diversified my income streams, the more secure and empowered I felt.

However, the journey to financial independence wasn't without its challenges. There were times when I doubted myself and my abilities. Businesses failed, investments didn't pan out, and setbacks seemed to be around every corner. But each failure was a lesson, and each setback provided an opportunity to grow.

Persistence was key. I refused to give up, even when things got tough. I adapted my strategies, learned from my mistakes, and kept pushing forward. This resilience paid off. Over time, I developed a keen sense of what worked and what didn't, and I became more efficient in my efforts.

One of the most significant shifts in my journey was learning to achieve balance. I realized that working myself to the bone wasn't sustainable. I needed to prioritize my well-being and find ways to work smarter. This meant delegating tasks, automating processes, and focusing on high-impact activities.

I started meeting regularly with a mentor. We worked on implementing systems and routines that optimized my productivity. This allowed me to achieve more in less time, freeing up space for relaxation and self-care. I learned to value my time and to invest it wisely, both in my professional and personal life.

As I achieved my financial goals, I felt a strong desire to give back. I wanted to empower others to achieve the same success. I began a nonprofit organization, Brighter View Foundation, inspiring entrepreneurs, sharing my experiences and insights with families like mine. I also started mentoring to support women pursuing life-changing career moves in business and social services.

Giving back has been one of the most rewarding aspects of my journey. It has allowed me to make a positive impact and to create a legacy of empowerment and success.

My journey to earning a six-figure income has been transformative. It has taught me the importance of investing in myself, embracing change, and persistently pursuing my goals. While I have achieved a level of financial success, the journey doesn't end here. I continue to seek growth and new opportunities, always striving to improve and evolve.

If you're reading this, know that achieving a six-figure income without sacrificing your well-being is absolutely possible. It requires a shift in mindset, a willingness to invest in yourself, and a commitment to working smarter. Surround yourself with supportive, like-minded individuals, and never stop learning and growing.

Your journey starts now. Believe in yourself, take action, and embrace the possibilities. Success is within your reach. Go out there and create the life you desire.

Favorite Quote

"Knowing is not enough; we must apply.
Willing is not enough; we must do."
— JOHANN WOLFGANG VON GOETHE

Recommended Affirmation

I am deserving of a life filled with joy and abundance. The only thing left to decide is my next best step forward.

Shantoya's Special Offer

Let me help you! This is just a small piece of a much bigger story that's still unfolding. Connect with me for more tips and tools to help balance your work-life harmony and take ACTION on your entrepreneurial journey! Visit www.ShantoyaNicole.com/sixfigurechicks to get started.

About Shantoya Nicole Thomas,

Founder/Executive Director Brighter View Foundation

Shantoya is a social entrepreneur with 20+ years in human services, driving social impact across industries. As Founder/Executive Director of Brighter View Foundation, she empowers families in the I/DD community. A proud mom and advocate for diversity, Shantoya ignites passion and change, fostering growth through her ventures in retail, health, transportation, and nonprofits. She enjoys fitness, arts, and travel with her family, leaving a lasting impact as a seasoned facilitator and mentor.

Silvia Hernandes's *Story*

Determined to be independent, I started working at the tender age of seventeen, despite my dad's will. Coming from a modest family, with my dad working tirelessly to afford private school fees until I graduated high school, the value of hard work and perseverance was etched into my very being from a young age. He wanted me to attend school full time, but I wanted to earn my own money!

I balanced working during the day and attending college at night to pay my own tuition, and of course, earn my own money. It took me five and a half years to graduate with a degree in Psychology, traveling to a different town every night to attend college. I knew early on that dealing with people's psyche was not for me. I wanted something more tangible. The brain was too complex for me to understand. I chose Organizational Behavior as a branch of Psychology to pursue as a career since I found human behavior easier to decipher and less complex to course correct. I was fascinated by the fact that body language and behavior can say so much about a person. This choice served as my main base to build my career in human resources.

I decided then to pursue an HR career in the corporate world. Even before starting to look for a job, I knew I had to differentiate myself from the competition to find a good opportunity. With my internship in HR, I learned that having fluency in English was an important skill. To achieve this, I prepared myself financially to move to London post-graduation to immerse myself in the English language and learn more about European culture two years before I graduated from college. I did not know anyone there, and it was my first time leaving my parents' home. The dream was much bigger than the fear, and so I landed in London to study and experience the unknown. After two years of hard work to pay for school, and a world of life experience, I went back to my home country–Brazil–with English certifications from Oxford and Cambridge Universities. I was ready then to start my career in a multinational organization.

My efforts paid off when I got my first job in HR in a great corporation; my fluency in English gave me the competitive advantage. I was right! Acquiring a skill that not very many candidates had at that time–early 90s–provided me huge leverage. The lesson was clear: leaving my family and friends behind, enduring hardship abroad, and working hard seven days a week enabled me to seize a multinational company opportunity back home, marking the start of my corporate journey as a distinctive candidate. Oddly enough, this corporation had its headquarters in France, and all employees had to learn the language to advance their career. Challenge accepted! After two years I became fluent in French too.

Promotions and growth followed as I continued to acquire more skills to reach the top of the ladder. I decided then to get an MBA, focusing on Human Resources. One more certification granted me more opportunity to grow and get recognition in the field. My career continued to flourish when I was faced with an opportunity to be a director, but an international HR certification was a requirement to get this job. As the position was part of a succession planning, I was given one year to complete and then get promoted. I started to apply for universities in California and got accepted by the University of California Los Angeles (UCLA) in 2002. I moved to the U.S. and attended the program full time as an international student. After earning the certification in HR, the idea was to go back home and get that Director job. What I did not know was that all international students were granted a one-year internship in the field of study in the U.S. That was a huge surprise!

All I wanted was to practice, get more experience and take this knowledge to Brazil. In looking for a job, I applied for a temporary position at Nestle headquarters in Los Angeles. As my resume already had ten years of international experience in Brazil, I was hired right away. The temporary job became full time with the opportunity to work in several different departments within HR. I embraced the challenges of the field, new laws, new processes and so much learning. After one year, I was so happy with my career that I decided to make the U.S. my home! Nestle became my work home for the next six years.

The promotions and opportunities continued to present themselves, such as when I got my first Director role and moved to Arizona. Seven months later, I faced the biggest challenge of my life—a cancer diagnosis with a rare genetic condition. I was caught by surprise. Fourteen months of treatment kept me away from work. I had several surgeries and couldn't do much on my own. I learned very quickly to be more grateful every day for being able to shower by myself. At that time, it was a challenge. After the doctor's release I started applying for jobs without success. My body was ready, but my head was not. After a year away from the market, my confidence got a little wobbly. Yet, I was determined to overcome all the challenges and be back in corporate America again.

A call came from a recruiter to participate in a process for a Chief Human Resources Officer role, the highest level of the profession. At that point I was already a very successful professional, and it could naturally be my next move. For a moment I thought that was too much for me. Afterall, I was in a director role for just seven months. Something inside me said, "Of course you can do this." So, I gave more meaning to this voice rather than the feeling of self-doubt. The recruiter told me my experience was everything they needed. After several interviews, I was offered the job, and I became the Chief HR Officer for the State of Arizona, in charge of more than 100 agencies, boards and commissions and leading close to 10,000 employees. Yes, I reached the TOP! And most importantly, in the same week I got the greatest news: I was cancer-free.

Working in government was a challenge. The rules are very different from the private sector, where I had been for almost twenty years. Yet, I am proud to say I achieved amazing results leading to an award from the Governor's office for one of the top five most impactful projects delivered that year. This project brought efficiencies and cost savings to the recruiting process involving the entire Administration.

After almost thirty years, I left the corporate world fully in 2022, transitioning to entrepreneurship with my company, Lean Human Resources Partners. The world of HR and Psychology taught me so much about the interface between people and business that I felt very equipped to serve as an advisor to small businesses and individuals in this field. During my tenure in HR, I always had a passion for helping others get promoted and have a fulfilling career. I successfully coached so many people that it became my next goal to provide my expertise to as many people as I can to find what makes them happy when it comes to their professional lives.

Running my own HR company and living the dream daily has been teaching me the most significant lesson: the journey is more important than the destination. Embracing the hurdles, celebrating the small wins and cherishing progress over perfection is the recipe for happiness. On top of that, I get to help people.

I invite you all to focus on the dream, but also cherish the journey. Challenges will always be there, and they are necessary to teach us resilience, forcing us to leave our comfort zone, encouraging change and conquering more. You are meant for more. Focus, determination, courage, action and progress. I promise you can achieve anything you want. Let's go and get it!

Favorite Quote

"Winners never quit. Quitters never win!"

— LISA NICHOLS

Recommended Affirmation

I am the architect of my success, empowering others with passion and confidence.

Silvia's Special Offer

Feeling stuck or frustrated in your current career? Silvia Hernandes offers you an exclusive opportunity to transform your career and achieve your dream goals. As a special gift, readers of this chapter can claim a free consultation with Silvia to start your journey from unhappiness to fulfillment. Visit www.leanhrpartners.net/sixfigurechicks to redeem your consultation today!

About Silvia Hernandes,

Founder - Lean Human Resources Partners

Silvia, originally from Brazil, has over 25 years of HR expertise, holding an MBA, two HR certifications, and a Lean Six Sigma Green Belt. She's worked with Fortune 500 companies and served as Chief of HR for the State of Arizona, earning an award for a groundbreaking recruiting project. In 2022, Silvia founded Lean Human Resources Partners to help small businesses and individuals unlock their true potential. She resides in Scottsdale, AZ.

Stephanie Russell's *Story*

I have always been a quick learner with an eagerness to excel in my career path, but if someone had told me in my twenties that I would be running a six-figure company that would grow nationally I would have laughed in their face. No way! That is never going to happen to me!

I had never considered the possibility of owning my own company. I had been trained to work for a hospital or healthcare organization that offered great benefits, while being a "loyal" employee until retirement. How about you?

I quickly learned that my income would be capped. I would work weekends and holidays and hope and pray that I would get my vacation requests granted. I worked long twelve-hour shifts that often turned into sixteen or twenty-four-hour shifts. Even as I worked my way up the ladder through leadership roles into higher paying positions, I was still falling into the same trap. I was working very hard, giving up time with my son, family, and friends, and reaping little to no financial rewards.

I was an owner's dream! I ran their organization, increased their profits, and walked away without a piece of the profit when they sold their business and retired to their dream house on the beach. Does this sound familiar?

As I entered my forties, I really began to think about my financial future and ability to retire before the age of 80! As an Executive Director in Hospice, I interviewed nurses for open positions and began to pay attention to the ages of nurses I was interviewing. I knew that I had to reconsider my path if I wanted to avoid working well into my golden years.

What was my retirement plan? Would I be able to retire? Passive income suddenly became very important to me. I needed to seriously consider how I could grow my own organization with the perks of ownership that also allowed me to continue with my passion...helping people.

I was raised in Indiana, and as a little girl I remember playing "Doctor" with my stuffed animals. I knew from a very young age that I wanted to be in the medical field and help people. As a teenager I was addicted to the TV show *Trauma in the ER* and was very drawn to emergency medicine and saving lives. I loved the idea of knowing what to do in any medical crisis to help someone in need. My first job was as a lifeguard and swim instructor. When I graduated high school, within a year I enrolled in my first nursing program.

I cleaned offices after school throughout the week and worked as a waitress on the weekends. I would soon learn that I made more money waiting on tables than I would make as a nurse. I was floored after spending a year in an advanced nursing program, working two jobs, studying until the wee hours of the morning, and learning that my first job in a hospital would only pay me $11/hour.

So, I continued my education and became a RN with a BSN. I obtained a specialty in Dialysis. I was finally making $30/hour. I felt like I had made it! But I quickly learned that I was still living paycheck to paycheck, unable to afford vacations, and working long shifts, overtime, and holidays and weekends. I also found myself in credit card debt like so many other young working professionals.

I eventually moved to Arizona to be closer to my family and began a career as a hospice nurse case manager. I was disappointed when my income did not change. I was offered the same hourly amount that I was making in Kentucky.

I was assigned a caseload of patients, generally ranging from ten to fifteen patients. I oversaw their care needs in their home, which as I learned, is where most people want to have their care provided. There really is nothing that compares to the comfort and safety that comes with being at home.

I learned my new role quickly and excelled within the organization. I was offered the Director of Nursing position within six months of starting my job. I was with this company for over five years, with an ending position of Executive Director. I had the opportunity to learn how to operate and grow a Hospice. I was very good at my role. BUT I was working seven days a week, constantly on call, and the backup nurse for all issues within the organization.

When we were short-staffed, I filled in. When nurses were on vacation, I took over their caseloads. I worked tirelessly the entire time I was employed, and at the end of the day I learned that I was disposable to the owners. While I was quadrupling their organization and running the day-to-day operations, they were making plans for their exit. I was fired after being a loyal employee for over five years, and they ended up selling their Hospice and retiring in their dream home on the beach.

No worries! I had a great resume with lots of experience. I could find another job with a new Hospice. And so, I did. I was recruited by another Hospice to be their Executive Director. I spent the first two months doing audits and realized that we had to clean house and hire new employees. We quickly began growing our census and improving the work environment.

This was the pivotal point in my career when I began to realize that *I was the talent*. I was able to grow the organization, develop relationships within the community, and hire talented healthcare professionals. Why am I doing this for another company AGAIN? I should be doing this for myself, right? There is a good chance your boss doesn't deserve you either. My bosses certainly didn't appreciate me or the explosive growth they obtained under my leadership.

While these thoughts were in the back of my mind, I became very passionate about the gaps in care for patients when they are discharged from the hospital setting. I was able to recognize why patients were failing at home and returning to the hospital within a short period of time after being discharged to their home. They were not getting the proper level of care in their home to be successful or age in place safely and avoid an unnecessary hospitalization.

I began meeting with other business owners and putting together a team of necessary resources for patients to receive the care they needed in their home to age in place safely. I would assess their needs and make the appropriate referrals to businesses to assist the families. This removed the burden of navigating the complex medical system and ultimately led to the launch of Concierge Senior Care Management.

This was the most exciting and scariest thing that I have ever done in my career. I went from receiving a reliable paycheck every two weeks, to relying on myself to create my income and success. This was terrifying! It was 2020. Was I really launching a business during the Covid-19 pandemic? Was this really the best time to launch a company?

The answer was YES! It was the perfect time. I had the ability to work PRN (as needed), which allowed me to pick up as much or as little work as I needed when I was available, with two different Hospices while I was building my business. Families needed my services more than ever to navigate their care in the medical system to age in place safely and avoid unnecessary hospitalizations.

Within one year I had more than replaced my income and was able to walk away from my PRN positions. This was the most exciting time in my career. I was able to hire and train my own employees and offer them a career from home making more money than they would make working with a physician group Monday through Friday.

What is more exciting than this? I am running a successful company that is thriving with happy employees and clients. I determine my business hours. I decide when I take my vacations. I no longer work on holidays or weekends. I have the flexibility to complete my work from anywhere. Aren't time freedom and financial success things we all deserve? How could it get better than this?

Well, I am happy to say that things do get even better than this! I am now helping Healthcare professionals to transition to enjoy time and financial freedom with their own successful ventures within the fastest growing "multi-trillion-dollar" healthcare industry. If you are a certified/licensed healthcare professional and you are seriously interested in time and money freedom, I'd be happy to speak with you and support your next successful steps.

As an option for the right person, I am now licensing my program to enable healthcare professionals across the United States to successfully launch a six-figure business of their own by completing a certification program to utilize my business model. I help healthcare professionals transition from employee to owner, running their own successful six-figure business.

Concierge Senior Care Management licensees will now be able to help countless families across the United States to navigate their care across the healthcare spectrum while aging in place safely and avoiding unnecessary hospitalizations.

I've heard many times that when you can turn your passion into a successful career, you will never work a day in your life. I now know the meaning of this. Life is good. I am blessed. There really is nothing more fulfilling than helping families navigate the very complex medical system to ensure their parents get the best care available when they need it most.

"I've shared the biggest stages in the world with the biggest names and I can tell you that Stephanie is truly a consummate professional and an incredible support to countless healthcare professionals seeking their freedom from the stress, strain, and lack of appreciation they experience on the job. Let Stephanie help you unlock the vault of opportunities with her experience and coaching."

— *JAMES MACNEIL,*
International Best-Selling Author and Founder of Verbal Aikido

Favorite Quote

"What separates talent from success is hard work."

— STEPHEN KING

Recommended Affirmation

I am worthy and deserving to receive my version of success in this life.

Stephanie's Special Offer

If you are a certified/licensed healthcare professional and you are seriously interested in time and money freedom, complete this brief questionnaire and I will be in touch with you. NurseIncCSCM.com

About Stephanie Russell,

Owner Concierge Senior Care Management

Stephanie Russell, RN, BSN, is the owner of Concierge Senior Care Management, offering a certification program for healthcare professionals to launch their own six-figure business. With 25 years of medical experience, she specializes in helping families with aging parents through in-home assessments and essential resources. Stephanie empowers healthcare professionals to improve home care, prevent hospitalizations, and navigate the medical system with ease. She's the upcoming author of *Planned Senior Parenthood* and *Nurse Inc.*

SIX-FIGURE CHICKS

Section 2

Overcoming Common Obstacles

In this section, we share our thoughts on how we overcame specific obstacles, challenges, and problems in our lives and our businesses. We've organized the advice and tips by topic, based on the type of challenge we had to overcome. Whether or not you have certain obstacles, we recommend reading through them all to glean advice that may apply to future challenges or other areas of your life.

Overcoming Unworthiness

Ania Kubicki writes: Throughout my career, I've faced countless challenges that tested my sense of worthiness. And yes, intellectually I know that the key to overcoming this lies in recognizing that worthiness is not defined by external validation but by inner resolve.

Yet, even now, years into my career, it takes conscious effort to remember to turn each setback into an opportunity to reaffirm value, not diminish it. This shift in perspective is crucial—without it, we risk internalizing failure instead of learning from it. True growth comes from seeing challenges as catalysts for self-worth, not as verdicts on our abilities.

In my journey to overcome a sense of unworthiness, I make a conscious daily effort to embrace everything that happens, knowing that resilience builds strength. I also surround myself with a supportive network that sees my potential, even when I doubt it.

I've also learned to celebrate small victories—I use them as stepping stones to larger success. My faith also helps me remember that worthiness isn't something we earn; it's inherent.

In moments of doubt, I remind myself why I started and the impact I've already made. Worthiness is about self-belief, persistence, and embracing the journey, not just the destination.

Overcoming Lack of Boundaries

Ania Kubicki writes: Setting boundaries became essential when I realized I couldn't serve everyone, especially those who drained my energy. I learned this the hard way during my tenure as president of a local business organization. People constantly sought my time, but many were more interested in using it for their benefit than contributing to the collective good. It was exhausting and unsustainable.

I had to change my mindset, recognizing that being a good person doesn't mean making time for everyone. Instead, I decided to play a game and see my life as if it was a country, with clear borders and entry requirements. Not everyone deserves a visa to my inner circle; only those who align with my values and contribute positively are allowed in.

This shift wasn't easy, but it was necessary. I became more discerning about who I let into my space, understanding that my time and energy are precious resources. Setting boundaries is about self-respect and protecting your well-being. It's about recognizing that you cannot pour from an empty cup. By creating this fun game of looking at myself as if I was a country, I've created a healthier, more balanced life where I can thrive and genuinely support those who truly matter. I am considering rolling this strategy out as an app. I think it is a good strategy that can help proactively protect everyone's energy and surroundings.

Kimberly Mitchell writes: It's important to set personal boundaries and prioritize your health first. If you are a mom, fill your mom cup first. As a business owner, be careful not to commit to too many networking meetings, board meetings, etc. Spreading yourself too thin makes it difficult to show up where it matters most.

As a mom, it's rare to fill your own cup first—until something happens and you feel burnt out. The first couple years of business I was definitely feeling the burnout. I overcommitted to too many networking events and didn't get up every day to journal, meditate, and exercise. Out of necessity, I figured out how to set boundaries and follow them.

It didn't happen overnight, but over time, I learned to limit my commitments. Now I refuse 90 percent of the time (within reason) to ever committing to being anywhere before 9 a.m. This way my me-time is protected and gets done before any shit hits the fan. I also only commit to two nights a week that are networking, board meetings or something work-related. Take baby steps with boundaries (i.e. start exercising 3 days a week, then gradually increase), and then eventually you'll create everyday habits.

Silvia Hernandes writes: Experiences where others take advantage of your willingness to help can serve as crucial lessons in setting boundaries. For your well-being, it's sometimes necessary to say no. Many people find it difficult to refuse requests due to a desire to please others or avoid conflict. However, consistently saying yes to avoid confrontation can become overwhelming and unsustainable.

People often avoid setting boundaries out of fear of disappointing others. Yet, establishing and maintaining boundaries is essential for our mental health. When you overextend yourself and can't meet all your commitments, the resulting sense of failure can negatively impact your mental state. Without boundaries, you risk becoming drained of your energy.

Always saying yes has its costs. By setting boundaries, you show respect for your own time and energy. When you uphold these limits—whether through saying no or renegotiating deadlines—you earn respect from others. It's important to remember that it's your responsibility to enforce your boundaries, not someone else's.

Stephanie Russell writes: Setting boundaries has always been an area that I've struggled with. I am DEFINITELY guilty of putting others' needs above mine both professionally and personally. As a nurse, my job is to help others. For the first three years after launching my company, I was available to my clients on the evenings, weekends, and sometimes even holidays, and I didn't ask for extra pay. They had access to my personal cell phone.

I have finally learned that I am just as important as the families I am helping. As a business owner, there is always something that needs to be done. BUT many of these things can wait. And my time is valuable, too.

I am now only available Monday through Friday from 9-5. I do not work on holidays or weekends. I hire professionals to do all the things I am not good at so that I can focus on my strengths and know that the work I've delegated will be handled effectively and professionally.

Once I finally set boundaries, life changed! I wish I had done this from the beginning. If you can't do it, delegate it.

Overcoming Doubt

Amber Harman writes: I am overcoming doubt this very moment. I honestly did not feel good enough to be in Mel's book. All of these women are extremely successful. They all own businesses and have teams working for them and with them. I admire each and every author in *Six Figure Chicks*. As I sit here, I struggle to see how I can even compete.

What's beautiful is that all these women have been supportive and encouraging. It's a blessing to be able to have a career, making six figures, and I don't own a business. I'm blessed to have a husband who pushed me to be brave enough to be an author in *Six Figure Chicks*. I am blessed to have Mel push me to own who I am and that I am good enough.

When you are doubting yourself, trust the people around you. They obviously see something in you amazing, and there is a reason for that. My support system gave me the strength to see that I earned this opportunity, and I will be forever grateful.

Ania Kubicki writes: Overcoming doubt is an ongoing journey for me. Doubts can be a healthy part of growth—they prompt us to check ourselves, evaluate our decisions, and consider alternative perspectives. They keep us grounded, ensuring we don't become complacent or overly confident.

Cheryl James writes: Starting my business felt like diving into the deep end of the pool without knowing how to swim (side note: I really can't swim). Doubt was ever-present, like an unwanted houseguest that just wouldn't leave. I remember staring at my first big project, thinking, "Can I really do this?" Spoiler alert: I could, but it took some serious mental gymnastics to get there.

Doubt constantly whispered in my ear, asking if I was making a mistake leaving my stable corporate job, especially being over forty. To combat this, I became my own cheerleader. I kept a journal of small victories, no matter how trivial they seemed. Got a positive client email? It went in the journal. Managed to balance my budget? Journal entry. These little wins piled up and soon outweighed the whispers of doubt.

Networking played a huge role too. I surrounded myself with other entrepreneurs also battling their inner critics. Misery loves company, but so does success! Sharing stories and laughs over our mutual imposter syndromes was incredibly therapeutic. We weren't alone in this, and neither are you.

In the end, it was about trusting the process and, more importantly, trusting myself. Doubt still pops in occasionally, but now it's more like an old friend who visits briefly and then leaves. And when it does, I remind myself of how far I've come—and how far I have yet to go.

Stephanie Russell writes: Self-doubt—we all have it! Some of us hide it better than others. Self-doubt almost made me an employee for life, working around the clock to build someone else's dream while helping them retire in their dream home on the beach.

Was I able to take the biggest risk in my career and leave my cozy and dependable paycheck every two weeks to build my dreams? It took some real soul searching to gather the courage to start my own company. I had to talk myself off the ledge for quite some time before pulling the trigger and "going for it!"

It was 2020 when I launched my company. We were in the middle of a pandemic. I was able to work as a consultant for one hospice and help see patients for two other hospices while I was building the framework of my business: website, business cards, and a business phone line and email. These things took time and money.

I worked tirelessly seven days a week. I had plenty of work, which helped ease my financial concerns, and I began networking and building my referral sources. I was able to build my web application with my proprietary assessment. This was very exciting! I was able to walk away from my PRN work as a Nurse in under a year. Success is the best way to overcome self-doubt. Small wins every day turn into success! I learned to celebrate every small win.

Overcoming Imposter Syndrome

Jenny DeBolt writes: We all experience imposter syndrome—every single one of us. Just knowing that helps me realign my thoughts when those feelings creep in. When imposter syndrome rears its ugly head, remind yourself that it's a normal part of the journey. Acknowledge the feeling, then move past the negative thoughts it brings.

Lucy Kairalla writes: I am very familiar with the pesky voices that flood the mind. I've had many moments when I wondered if I deserved success or whether I was working hard enough. I thought I was alone in this, but as I met more and more successful businesswomen, I realized this is much more common than I would have ever imagined. This is true among even the most accomplished.

What most surprised me, however, is that what I thought would be my biggest weakness and hindrance to success became my greatest strength.

I am from Brazil and so my native language is not English. A reasonable assumption is that this would exclude me from starting a marketing career in America and would certainly cripple any hoped-for success. The truth is, I was so paranoid about potential grammar mistakes and unclear language in my deliverables that it ended up helping me be even clearer.

The fact is that clarity in marketing is everything and if a cavewoman can't understand the writing on the page, you're going to lose the sale. As a business owner from another country and culture, I represent that cavewoman. If you're losing me, you're likely losing 80 percent of your audience. My own need to understand plain language has turned my initial weakness for English into a critical eye for clarity. This is the superpower I now use to run a successful marketing business.

If you allow it, feelings of inadequacy will plague you. You are not alone when you feel this way. Learning how to turn your biggest weakness into your greatest strength isn't something an imposter can do, and this thought helps me remember how far I've come.

Stephanie Russell writes: Imposter Syndrome is a real thing! I struggled with my identity as a business owner for at least my first two years of ownership. My identity had always been an employee. I had become accustomed to having someone in a higher position than me to refer to when there was an issue or concern from a patient or a referring organization.

While I knew that I was the talent at the organizations I had worked for, it was a difficult transition. Self-doubt crept in! I found myself questioning my own abilities when I was doing presentations and networking. Will people believe in me? Will people refer their clients to me? Will organizations refer their patients to me? What if I can't handle it? Will I be as successful as other businesses? Do I really have what it takes?

As time went on these feelings began to fade. I began to believe in myself and my leadership abilities. I had done this successfully for other companies for over two decades, and my patients got the absolute best care from me. I ensure that my clients have the best solutions to age in place safely and avoid unnecessary hospitalizations. I am an expert, and families need my guidance to navigate the complex medical system.

Overcoming Fear of Failure

Ginger Clayton writes: Fairly early on I realized that I often was not moving forward with a new idea because I was afraid of what the failure might be. Would it cost too much money? Would it cost employee jobs? Would I end up on a street corner with my five kids holding a sign, "will work for food?" That last one seems so dramatic, but yet my mind always went there.

I realized without some of these big risks there would not be big rewards, and I had to get out of my own way. I know that I do better with a plan so I would gather a team and review all possibilities, good and bad. We would run a proforma and an ROI (Return on Investment) and move forward if we felt that the risk was worth it. I typically like to try a beta version first. For instance, when first starting the moving company, we hired subcontractors and rented trucks. Once we felt confident in our sales projections, we began hiring employees and buying trucks. This risk alone tripled our revenue in the first year, taking us from $1M to $3M!

Lucy Kairalla writes: This is another thought spiral trap that can keep us from making decisions and taking action. There are endless fears about stepping away from a secure paycheck, going into debt for business, thinking about what family and friends might think about my decisions, and how this could affect my career in the long term. The list goes on and the emotional toll and stress this can wreak on your mental health is no joking matter.

The best advice I got to combat the fear of failure was from a friend who said, "If you don't start you've already failed." I keep this one close as it relates to countless areas of life and business.

Another thing that has helped me with this is knowing that if I don't do it {insert fear}, I will always wonder what would have happened if I had. I know I'd feel miserable working a regular job being assigned tasks and expected to follow the rules of that particular organization. I'd be stuck doing things that benefited that company and the owners of that company instead of having some control over my work and being able to pour into a team that I put together.

Shantoya Nicole Thomas writes: To overcome the fear of failure, I started educating myself more. I read self-help books, attended free workshops, and networked with local business owners who had walked similar paths. One tool that helped immensely was creating a plan then following up with a mentor that helped turn those plans into actionable steps. It wasn't just about mapping out finances—it was about setting clear, achievable goals that kept me focused and motivated.

Silvia Hernandes writes: To conquer the fear of failure, I devote myself to seeking knowledge and extensive reading. I recognize that there's no need to reinvent the wheel. By identifying individuals who have managed to overcome their own fears of failure, I learn from their experiences and apply their strategies to my own life. This approach has been so effective that today, I can confidently say, "I have conquered the fear of failure."

In both my professional and personal life, I take action without knowing whether my efforts will lead to success or failure. However, if I do encounter failure, I simply adjust my course and explore a different path. I believe that not trying would lead to greater regret than failing. Each failure serves as a guide, revealing the right direction to take. I perceive failure as constructive.

Even the most successful individuals have faced numerous failures, which have helped them carve unique paths toward success. I have learned that failure is, in fact, essential. I no longer wish to avoid it; instead, I embrace it as a fundamental part of life and success. Failure helps us discover what doesn't work, making our journey a series of trials and errors. I strongly advocate for mirroring the practices of trusted, successful people. Learn from them, and always seek knowledge.

Stephanie Russell writes: As a single mother in my forties, I convinced myself that failure was not an option. I had to succeed. It may take me longer than I would like to build my business and replace my income, but I knew that I would eventually succeed. I had the passion and the drive, I just needed to make it work.

I had done this successfully for other companies, it was time to do it for myself. And I could always go back to being an employee, right? I had a great resume! If I needed to get a job I could. This is what drove me to succeed. I knew that my days of being an employee were over. I simply could not fathom being an employee any longer.

The thought of working for another company, asking for time off, working on holidays, working overtime, and being on call were enough to ignite my passion and drive to succeed. The fear of failure is what gave me the strength and determination to work tirelessly until I was able to replace my income, hire employees, and grow my business.

Overcoming What Held Me Back

Cassobin (Cassie Velasquez & Robin O'Shea) writes: What is holding you back from taking your business to the next level? When we thought about this as business partners, we realized what was holding us back was having the ability to relinquish control. Seeking external support and help is critical. You can't be the best at everything. Know your strengths and be willing to engage with a business mentor or coach who can provide personalized advice, accountability and support.

As business partners, we have identified in each other what our personal strengths are, and then capitalized on them. It took us over a year in owning the business to realize that we needed to build a team around us with strengths where we were lacking. That has catapulted us to another level of success.

The other critical piece that was holding us back was committing as business partners to continuous learning and personal development. Always stay curious and open to new ideas and approaches. Taking time to review what's working and what's not, and then making necessary adjustments will help you overcome the barriers that have been holding you back and set a clear path towards achieving success in your business.

Jenny DeBolt writes: I used to believe that if I wasn't bringing in a steady paycheck from an employer, I was failing at life. Now, I realize that was a limiting belief. I'm not saying that working for someone or having a steady income is a bad thing, but it's important to ask yourself: What are you doing to truly serve the world? We are meant to be so much more than just a paycheck.

Monica May-Dunn writes: In my career, the fact that I did not speak up to the company founder held me back the most because he didn't want me going anywhere. I wish I would have been given the opportunity to buy the company earlier. I wish I would have been tougher and spoken to the founder directly ten years ago.

What held me back most in that situation was my reluctance to face confrontation. To overcome being held back, speak up! Never be afraid to speak up. I was raised in a "be seen, not heard" environment, so I was very shy growing up. Up until just a few years ago, I had been very shy. It is only recently that I have realized that my voice does matter and it's important for me to use it!

Overcoming Lack of Confidence

Ginger Clayton writes: When I have been nominated for awards, it was always exciting and also nerve-racking. I thank my mom for getting me into competitive dance and entering me in pageants when I was young. I was very shy, and these exercises taught me how to overcome this. I envision what success looked like including the smallest of details from hair/makeup, costume and the walk to the stage. Then I pictured my dance performance going off without a hitch. This would allow me to throw my shoulders back, hold my head up high and move forward.

Throughout the business award process, not only is there an extensive written portion but there is also an intense in-person interview in front of a panel of judges. I remember that in the beginning I was so focused on winning. Yes, that may have been my competitive nature, and I was mostly worried about disappointing my family and my team. I had made it to the finalists round and had to prepare an acceptance speech in case I won. I was struggling with confidence and what I should say. A dear friend and mentor, Eileen Rogers, gave me the best advice: It is not about winning, you are already a winner at this point in the process. It is less about what you "have" to say, it is what you "get" to say.

Even being an author in this book, I immediately went back to what she told me. What do I get to say that could help others, instead of being stalled by fear. When I position it this way, I talk about serving because I am passionate about that and it ties back to my personal mission to "create a fever to serve." When you feel insecure in a situation, draw on your power and what gives you strength, then you will find your voice.

Lisa Riley writes: Confidence is a powerful trait, but overcoming a lack of it can be a significant challenge. In my journey, I discovered that building confidence starts with small steps. Initially, I struggled with self-doubt, and I was hesitant to speak up or take risks. However, I gradually began to push myself out of my comfort zone.

I started by setting small, achievable goals. Each success, no matter how minor, boosted my confidence. I also learned the importance of self-affirmation. By reminding myself of my strengths and past achievements, I slowly built a more positive self-image.

Seeking feedback from trusted friends and mentors was another crucial step. Their constructive criticism and encouragement helped me see my potential from a different perspective.

Additionally, I embraced failure as a learning opportunity rather than a setback. Each mistake taught me valuable lessons and strengthened my resilience.

Over time, these practices transformed my mindset. I became more assertive, willing to take on challenges, and less afraid of failure. Building confidence is an ongoing process, but with perseverance and self-compassion, I have come to believe in my abilities and trust my judgment.

Overcoming Self-Sabotage

Jenny DeBolt writes: Don't listen to that negative-Nancy voice listing all the reasons you can't succeed. Learn to put her in her place and respond with confidence: 'Whatever, Nancy. Watch this. I am amazing!' And if your name is Nancy, feel free to pick a different name—ha!

Monica May-Dunn writes: Self-sabotage is real; I often talk myself out of things even though I know I can do them. Getting the support of my family and peers has been critical in new endeavors. When you don't think you can do something, it's essential to have your peers—people you respect and network with—build you up and support you. Networking and talking with people I trust has been instrumental in overcoming self-sabotage for me.

I also listen to a lot of leadership books that help me overcome things like self-sabotage.

Continuing to educate yourself, read books, take classes, and take leadership training all help you overcome the tendency to self-sabotage. The more you learn, the more you grow into a person who values herself and her worth, and the less likely you are to act in a self-sabotaging way.

Overcoming Gender Biases

Lisa Riley writes: When I began my teaching career at a university, two of my colleagues had already been teaching there since the year I was born! One held a PhD and the other a master's degree. Despite my qualifications, students consistently referred to me as "Ms." while both male professors were always called "Dr."

One of my mentors offered me invaluable advice: "Lisa, you never know if students are calling you 'Ms.' out of ignorance or malice. Always assume ignorance and be as graceful as the situation allows. In private, you can explain the significance of a doctorate and the title it entails, as they may not understand the distinction. In public, remember that you are both a 'Dr.' and a 'Ms.', so let it roll off your shoulder to avoid embarrassing the person."

This perspective helped me navigate gender biases with grace. By assuming ignorance rather than malice, I maintained my professionalism and used these moments as teaching opportunities. Over time, this approach not only helped correct misconceptions but also reinforced my role and respect.

Monica May-Dunn writes: Just today I had lunch with a company president, and out of the blue he said, "You're just so beautiful!" I thought, 'Thank you for the compliment, but are you listening to anything I'm saying? Getting men to take me seriously in a predominantly male industry is a challenge. Men commenting on a woman's looks instead of the subject we're here to talk about is a common issue. How do I handle it? I simply accept the compliment and then change the subject, such as, "That's very kind of you, I appreciate that. Now let's discuss..." Firm redirection is key.

I find that men in business often see superficial things about women instead of seeing the depth. It takes a lot of patience to consistently show up in the face of this gender bias. That said, I'm in an upcoming magazine issue that features fifty women in real estate. Women are being recognized more and more, and we need to celebrate it! It's important for women in business to share our stories and lift each other up. The more we do, the more men will respect us and take us seriously.

Overcoming Social Expectations

Cassobin (Cassie Velasquez and Robin O'Shea) writes: It is uncommon for teachers to leave the classroom to start their own business. Society expects educators to dedicate thirty-plus years in the classroom and then retire with their hard-earned pension. Certainly, leaving the classroom is more prevalent now due to low compensation and other related stressors, but colleagues move to educational support companies that offer better pay and reliable retirement programs.

When we decided to leave our district positions to start our business, we were met with many shocked faces and questions like, "What about your retirement?" "How are you going to survive?," and "Why would you throw your career away?" Those were hard questions to answer as we knew we were putting a lot on the line. But in true "Cassobin" form, we approached these doubts and cautionary notes with measured decision-making strategies and a lot of courage... the result was outstanding! In fact, we doubled revenue in the first two years and continue to expand!

The take-away here is to be aware of societal expectations as they can provide insights that you may need to consider. But also, if you have a passion and a plan, there are no limits or constraints you cannot overcome!

Lisa Riley writes: Growing up, I, along with many others, assumed I would get married and have children. However, my path took a different turn when I decided to attend graduate school. During orientation, I was greeted with the disheartening remark, "Happy people don't belong here; they should seek jobs as flight attendants."

In that moment, I resolved to prove that I did belong, regardless of their perceptions.

Determined to maintain my positive attitude, I navigated through both my master's and doctoral programs. I embraced the challenges and changes in expectations, finding joy in my academic journey and personal growth.

Throughout this time, I also celebrated my friends' milestones, serving as a bridesmaid ten times. While my life diverged from the traditional path I once envisioned, I realized that success and happiness come in many forms. By staying true to myself and defying societal expectations, I achieved my academic goals and discovered a deeper sense of fulfillment.

Overcoming Building a Support Network

Jenny DeBolt writes: It is essential to cultivate the right environment around you—starting with your relationships. If there's someone in your life who consistently brings negativity, complains, or drains your energy, it might be time to gently weed them out. You don't need to make a grand statement or take obvious action. Instead, consider gradually reducing the texts, phone calls, or visits. By tapering off these interactions, you can make the shift more subtle, minimizing any discomfort or confrontation. This process isn't always easy, but it's necessary for your growth and well-being.

Surround yourself with people who inspire you, challenge you, and help you grow. Keep relationships that you admire, not out of obligation or comfort, but because they genuinely enrich your life. Choosing your tribe is a crucial life skill, yet it's one that many of us are never taught. Take the time to nurture relationships that align with your values and aspirations. In doing so, you'll create a life where positivity, learning, and mutual support can flourish.

Lucy Kairalla writes: Building and maintaining a supportive network for business is crucial for success. Many business owners come at this from a 'leads' angle, thinking this is the main reason to build a network. While leads are important and necessary for building a business, it's essential to build on a strong foundation you can access when you have the need. Business is hard! The daily struggles go on and on, and if you don't have a system of support you will eventually burn out. This is especially true in the beginning stages.

One thing I did in the early stages of my startup was to join Vistage. Having regular access to a peer group of CEOs I could go to for advice and guidance was one of the best decisions I made. Here's the thing, it wasn't cheap. But I decided to invest in myself and my business because I knew that the support and mentorship you get from this kind of support network is unparalleled. This has proven to be the case for my business so I will always recommend a startup taking this action early.

If I can leave you with a golden nugget for this one, I'd say, "Your network is your net worth." Build a strong one!

Stephanie Russell writes: I had been a nurse in Arizona for ten years, so I had a solid network. But I must admit, I was nervous about how they would react to the news that I was launching my own company. Would they have as much faith in me as I had in myself?

I immediately began contacting everyone I knew to inform them of my new business and share my services so that I could be added to their referral platform. I started a networking group with my closest friends in business that eventually grew from eight people to well over fifty. It was very casual.

We would meet monthly at a restaurant to have a bite to eat and a cocktail. It grew organically! I wanted a networking group that was focused on relationship-building as opposed to something that was structured. After all, friends refer to friends! As it turns out, many other business professionals were looking for something just like this!

I also began calling on organizations to send them my information and schedule presentations for their teams. My presentations changed over time. I was very medical with my terminology, and I quickly realized that I had to change my verbiage to match the needs of my audience. This took time, and it is something I continue to work on.

While building my network seemed daunting in the beginning, over time it began to feel less intimidating. My network began to introduce me to their network, and my referral list began to grow. I also started to get referrals from friends and family of my clients, and this is the highest compliment in business.

Overcoming Lack of Biz / Family Life Balance

Betsy LaVoie writes: The idea of balance often implies equality—equal time, energy, and attention across all areas of life. As a professional woman aiming to excel as a CEO for our Chamber of Commerce, a Managing Director for our Foundation, a devoted mother of two, a loving girlfriend, and a homemaker, I've learned that balance doesn't come from equal distribution. I've never believed in the concept of "quality time" with children, seeing it as an excuse for not spending enough time with them. To achieve the balance I seek, I use various strategies.

One effective method is combining time with chores. Instead of multitasking for its own sake, I engage in simple tasks like folding laundry or mopping floors with my kids. During this time, we share our "Peach and Pit"—the best and worst parts of our day. This conversation happens during dinner if we can, or whenever we find a moment, ensuring we always connect.

Another strategy is setting hard stops for school pick-ups and drop-offs. While others could do this, I prioritize it. About 10 percent of the time, work conflicts prevent me, but 90 percent of the time, I'm there to wish them a great day and welcome them back after school.

Ginger Clayton writes: When I was a young rising manager in corporate America, in a male-dominated industry, I had a strong desire to have a great career and to also have a great family life. I was working many late nights and really struggling to find that balance, when an older male manager caringly told me, "Sweetheart, you have to pick one or the other, a family or a career, you just can't have both." I thought that was ridiculous and was determined that I would figure it out someday.

Becoming a business owner was how that happened, though I still struggled with balance in the early years. I created my list of roles: wife, mother, daughter, business owner, Christian, community servant, etc. I created these roles in my Outlook calendar, and everything got assigned a color. I studied how I was spending my time, and this gave me a great visual. I noticed there was no "blue" for my wife color. I had multitasking time with my husband, Joe, at work at kids' sports, charity events and clients' dinners, but there was no dedicated time for the two of us. Joe and I established a weekly date night because of that and continue that to this day. You can learn a lot by studying yourself!

As a business owner, I could bring my baby to work somedays, though this came with its own challenges too. I could leave early for my kids' school room-mom duties and finish work later in the evening. I found that not everything had to be in perfect balance all of the time for me to feel that I was being successful in all of my roles. Some weeks may have had a heavier load of activities within my mom role, another week in my wife role, community service, work activities, etc. I found that as long as I took "turns" over time, I felt a sense of balance and less of the plates that I was spinning fell.

Kimberly Mitchell writes: I don't believe there actually is a balance of business and family life. Work, and life, comes in waves that can be fairly consuming at times. When we are too focused on balance within a day or even a week, we can get really frustrated, upset or resentful.

There will be days or weeks where work is the main focus, and others that are more family-focused. It's not a straight line. I think having daily and quarterly goals are very important, however, you can get pretty overwhelmed if you try to focus on work-life balance. Rather than push yourself to do the same number of hours for work, family and self, just accept that life is messy.

Instead of trying to achieve work-life balance, set boundaries with your business and family. This way you aren't consumed by one or the other too much on a regular basis. For example, I'll have a holiday planned *after* the holiday so I have my own time. I also put every exercise class, every morning activity, every hair appointment, everything I do on my calendar. It all gets booked at my previous appointment so nothing else gets booked over. It's important for self-care.

Stephanie Russell writes: Owning a business and being a single mom is a challenge! The needs of my family come first, which meant that I had to work late into the evenings, early in the morning, and over the weekends to complete necessary work. In the beginning, this was a juggling act to say the least! And exhausting!

But I knew that my hard work and long hours would pay off in the end. I knew that I had to grow my business to the point where I could hire employees to complete the work while also generating an income for myself. In the beginning I wore all the hats!

Giving these hats away one at a time was one of the coolest things in business! Passive income for myself while creating opportunities for others to work from home was my driving factor. This is why we go into business for ourselves, right? We create opportunities for others while creating time to do the things we are most passionate about.

For me, I wanted to have the time freedom that comes with a passive income. I desperately wanted to attend all his sporting and school events without having to work late into the evening to get the work completed. I wanted to plan special vacations for us while knowing the work would be completed while I was away.

I gave myself two years after launching my business to reach this goal. I had a vision board, and this was number one on my list. I am happy to say that I accomplished this goal!

Overcoming Not Owning Your Accomplishments

Ginger Clayton writes: We were very blessed to be named as recipients for many business awards. I often struggled with this as my inner shy girl would surface and I didn't want to appear to be boasting when people would ask about our accomplishments. Another great mentor, Rena Huber, was the first one to nominate us for a few awards. She said that they are a great experience and great free PR. She was right!! We ended up on a roll and in the Business Journal fairly frequently—so much so that people often called me the "darling of TBJ."

I realized that owning these accomplishments was a testament to all of our employees who work so hard and do such an amazing job. These awards also help our sales team position us in a great light as companies love to do business with award-winning companies. This helped me to own our accomplishments. I will own my own accomplishments, however so many of our awards are for the company and are because of the amazing team members that I have surrounding me.

Lisa Riley writes: I've been fortunate to receive many awards, yet I often find it difficult to share my accomplishments with others. I wonder if this reluctance stems from my experience as a middle child, where I didn't want to outshine my siblings. Alternatively, it could be a reaction to those who frequently boast about their achievements, a behavior I've always wanted to avoid.

Despite my hesitation, I recognize that acknowledging and sharing my successes is important. My family (parents, siblings, aunts, uncles, husband, cousins) have always been proud of me, and of each other, regardless of what we achieved.

Over time, I've realized that owning my accomplishments is not about boasting but about acknowledging my hard work and growth. It's a way to inspire others and show gratitude for the support I've received. Sharing my achievements doesn't diminish the successes of others; instead, it contributes to a culture of mutual encouragement.

Embracing my accomplishments involves a balance of humility and confidence. It's about understanding that being proud of my achievements is not selfish. By owning my successes, I can continue to grow, motivate others, and contribute positively to my personal and professional communities.

Overcoming Lack of Capital

Stephanie Russell writes: As a nurse, I was able to work PRN so that I could continue to get a paycheck while having the flexibility to work as much or as little as I needed to while launching my company. While I was working long hours, seven days a week, I was thankful to have the flexibility.

Many medical professionals can work three 12-hour shifts every weekend and get the benefits of full-time pay while having Monday through Friday off to build their own business. I was a hospice nurse at the time, and I had more work than I could ask for. I was able to work as many hours as I needed when I had the time to work. Having this flexibility was critical to my success.

I did not have a lot of money in the bank, and I didn't want to go through the savings that I had. I was able to pay for my business expenses without touching my savings account. This was a big deal for me. As my business grew, I was eventually able to reduce my PRN hours. And one day I realized that I could walk away from the PRN hours completely.

This was the first milestone in my business. I celebrated this win with a gift for myself. It is very important to celebrate the wins no matter how big or small they are. Celebrating the wins makes hitting your goals that much more awesome!

Overcoming the Fear of Asking for Help

Cassobin (Cassie Velasquez and Robin O'Shea) writes: Asking for help for us, in the beginning of our journey, was a fear because we assumed that people would judge us or peg us as not being competent. They would think that we were asking because we didn't know what we were doing. We soon realized that instead of fearing judgment, we needed to focus on the value of the information or assistance we were seeking. When we shifted our thinking to asking so that it would help us achieve our goals or solve our problems, a new world emerged.

In our business, we teach the importance of asking questions because it generates collaboration, which as a result, generates new, creative ideas. When we began asking questions of our consultants, those people with boots on the ground in the field, many new ideas emerged. Another added bonus that we didn't anticipate was that it gave them a feeling of ownership in what they were doing.

Embrace the idea that asking questions and making requests is part of the learning process. Each question or request is an opportunity for growth.

Kimberly Mylls writes: When it comes to asking, I always think first: it is better to regret something you have done than something you have never done. Another way to overcome the fear of asking is to visualize the worst-case scenario, then the best case scenario and the most likely. When you can see those three scenarios, it can alleviate the fear. Learn to be clear on what you're asking for, and the more you ask the more confidence you build.

Remember even when someone says no - it might be no for now. There are many times in my career clients said no and six months or even a year later came back and said yes.

Overcoming the Fear of Taking Risks

Ginger Clayton writes: I tend to be more of a cautious person fiscally, though I am also an adrenaline junkie at heart. I would say that I have a medium risk tolerance, but that has grown, and I am more comfortable taking bigger risks now. I found that when I listened to my gut things worked out. Often when I ignored my instincts something went awry.

I had to gain confidence with successes in taking smaller risks, and also acknowledge there can be success in the failures. Failures can be gifts that push you to something greater. When I had failed and rebounded, I learned that the sky did not fall and all would be ok. I am naturally pretty resilient, so that helped a great deal as well. I gained confidence that I could rebound in the wake of a failure. There was important information that was gained and could be used to move in a different, and often better, direction.

Jenny DeBolt writes: I love setting goals with others, they almost always think I'm out of my mind with the goals I propose, especially in a team setting. My motto is GO BIG! Take risks! Don't settle for comfort. Too often, we set goals and take action in ways that feel safe and familiar. It's time to break free from that. Stop playing it safe and push beyond your comfort zone.

Lucy Kairalla writes: We all know that no growth happens in the comfort zone. If you're an entrepreneur, you're a natural risk taker.

You took the first risk to start your own business in the first place. That is no small deal. It would be nice to say that at some point your business will level off and the discomfort will disappear into your memory, but this is not reality.

Whether you are trying to decide on a new tech platform, choosing the best accountant, hiring new team members, or betting on a new marketing strategy, you have to decide to jump. You can run a conservative business if you want but you'll never grow past a certain point. If you want to scale, you have to keep taking risks. It will always be uncomfortable. The ability to keep taking risks is essential to being an entrepreneur.

When I'm getting ready to try something new, I go on a fact-finding mission. I talk to as many people as possible, and do my research, so I can be confident I'm making the most informed decision. It's not completely risk-free, but no decision will be, and it helps to alleviate the anxiety that inherently comes with risk.

Shantoya Nicole Thomas writes: Taking risks is an inherent part of growth, both in life and business. I realized that my fear of judgment was holding me back from taking risks. In business, this meant not speaking up in meetings or avoiding new ventures because I feared failure. I started practicing self-compassion and mindfulness, which helps me accept vulnerability as part of the human experience. By journaling, I became more aware of my fears and learned to embrace them. I still work on this, especially in moments when I feel exposed. However, I've grown more comfortable with vulnerability and now view it as a strength. I am who I am and that is what makes me. Taking risks and learning from failure has given me many wonderful life experiences.

Overcoming Feeling the Need to be Perfect

Amber Harman writes: Being a Virgo may play into my role of needing to feel perfect. I believe my need to feel perfect ultimately came from my household and environment from the moment I was brought into this world. I have a narcissistic parent, and nothing ever felt good enough. My intentions were always geared by wanting their approval and a need to feel loved.

I remember in elementary school, during Christmas, they would have this little shop set up, so that you could get your family a gift. It was all junk, but at eight years old it was stuff I thought was cool. I used all the money I had saved up and got my parent this "cool" pen with a pom pom attached. I remember even now; how proud I was that I got my parent a gift and how excited I was. I couldn't wait to give this gift. Christmas Day came, and I could barely hold back my excitement. As I watched my parent open it, I felt like I could burst. The look on their face was filled with disappointment, followed by, "This is it? This is what you got me?" as it was tossed aside. I was crushed.

It took me twenty-six years before I realized that I was not the problem. That's a long time trying to "win" love and approval. It's a huge accomplishment for me to be at a point in my life where I truly understand that I cannot control other people's feelings and behavior. You have to love yourself and know that you are enough.

Ginger Clayton writes: I was a competitive tap dancer as a young girl with aspirations of becoming a Radio City Rockette. Good thing that life took me a different direction, because at 5'0" I would not have been tall enough! In all of my preparations for competitions, I was always practicing to be perfect. What happens when you are perfect? You get a lot of praise; you win awards, and you advance to the next level.

I was very driven, and I am still a recovering perfectionist, however I worked with my Executive Coach, Heather Story, and she helped me tremendously with this. One key thing that she had me do was to have a separate piece of note paper and write down every time my inner gremlin reared its head, you know that negative voice in your head that tells you things like: "you aren't good enough, you don't know what you are doing, who do you think you are?" I was surprised how many times my gremlin was being sassy in a day! She then had me rephrase the sassy gremlin talk with positive affirmations such as: "You've got this! You can figure this out! You know this! You can do hard things!" It sounds so simple; knowledge is power and studying yourself and making a minor change can be profound.

I also found that this was a major reason why I took a long time to complete certain things. I became comfortable with the fact that getting something done was better than it being perfect; it was too much of a waste of time fussing over the font in a presentation, or the perfect image, etc. I also learned that my "good enough" was most people's perfect.

Jenny DeBolt writes: Here's the thing about perfection: it doesn't exist. When you constantly strive for perfection, you end up spinning your wheels and eventually crashing and burning. Many of us fall into this cycle repeatedly, not realizing the harm we're doing to ourselves. But bonus—it's our imperfections that make us truly wonderful.

Silvia Hernandes writes: To overcome the need for perfection, I shift my mindset. I recognize and accept that nobody is perfect, and no one ever will be. There are always areas where we can improve. Even if I aim for perfection, there will be aspects I'm good at and others where I'm not as proficient. By striving to do my best without the illusion of perfection, I find myself in a healthier mindset.

I remind myself that I'm not alone in this; all human beings are in the same situation, and this shared experience makes me feel secure. It brings peace of mind to know that it's okay to make mistakes. We are all in this together. Trying too hard to be perfect often appears forced and unnatural. Perfection

Overcoming Being Labeled As Too Emotional

Cassobin (Cassie Velasquez and Robin O'Shea) writes: As special educators working with special education staff and families, we bring empathy and emotion to our business. While these are critical characteristics when working in a human industry, it can also be a barrier when making decisions and operating a successful business enterprise. So how have we balanced the two? We follow a multi-dimensional framework for our organizational success and address each equally.

The three dimensions to our success are: maintaining a balanced focus on business processes, relationships, and results. Here is an example of each.

- Process: these are the structures we have created to operate an efficient business—this is the "how" we achieve our results;
- Relationships: these are the quality connections and trusting partnerships with our clients and consultants. Relationships help to identify diverse needs and create new opportunities; and
- Results: these are the specific desired outcomes or the "what" we want to accomplish. We always start with this in mind and then plan how to get there.

By focusing equally on each of these dimensions, we can balance our emotions with strategic processes and achieve positive results.

Overcoming Not Valuing Your Work Correctly

Cassobin (Cassie Velasquez and Robin O'Shea) writes: We did not get into the field of education because we were driven by money... I think that goes without saying. As we all know, educators are overworked and underpaid. We got into education, especially the field of special education, because we wanted to work with students with disabilities. We wanted to make a difference in their lives and their family's lives.

When we were blessed with the opportunity to be business owners of a company that does just that, our mindset had to shift. It did not shift from still wanting to make a difference, as that is still at the core of what we do, but we had to shift into a business mindset. We were faced with the challenge of remembering that we now must balance our desire to help with making sure we are not giving away our services, otherwise we will not stay afloat. Finding that balance is a daily struggle for us. We have developed a mantra... stay humble and kind, and don't get greedy.

Kimberly Mylls writes: Knowing how to price your products and services can be so challenging. I have worked with so many businesses who give way too much away for free! I used to do the same thing! I would spend an hour on the phone giving business advice for free. I would put together comprehensive strategy proposals only for a client to say they were going to do it on their own. I made two big adjustments.

The first adjustment was that I started charging for my time. If someone wanted to "pick my brain" they could do so at my hourly rate. The second adjustment was that I started charging for a proposal. If they accepted the proposal, they could apply the proposal fee to the project. If they decided no, I was still compensated for my proposed strategy. A couple things happened. I started attracting my ideal client, and those clients saw value and became long term clients. I adopted the philosophy of: "You can pick my brain after you pick your payment plan!"

Overcoming Unfavorable Environments

Betsy LaVoie writes: In today's politically-charged society, our organization, like many advocacy groups, frequently faces attacks. When I first took on the leadership role, I had to address issues and decisions made by previous leadership, sometimes from twenty to thirty years ago, which some people still resented. My guiding principle is to treat others as I would like to be treated, regardless of how they treat me. Therefore, I strive to be a positive force, providing accurate and truthful information backed by data. I do not respond to attacks or negativity but continue to focus on the work I was hired to do.

No matter how I am treated, I always greet people with a hello and a smile. This may seem basic, but sincerely greeting someone as you would like to be greeted, even after they have attacked you on social media, for example, is a challenging but worthy endeavor. To maintain a positive and sincere attitude, I often remind myself out loud, "I treat others as I would like to be treated, not as they are currently treating me!" Saying these words out loud provides the affirmation I need to remain positive and professional.

Kimberly Mylls writes: Being in an unfavorable environment can take its toll. I have worked for horrible bosses, been around toxic employees and been in places where I have no privacy and feel stuck. It's one of the reasons I love working from home and why I chose to be an entrepreneur. I would sit in my car five minutes before I walked into a toxic workplace and practice gratitude while listening to my favorite music. I focused on having a positive mindset throughout the day. When things would spiral, I would look for the positive. When that didn't work, I would take a break, get outside, do anything to change my state or physical environment.

I also had clear goals. Setting clear boundaries is going to give you some peace of mind. In challenging times I would keep asking myself, "What can I learn from this, and what are the opportunities?" I practiced keeping a positive mindset and focusing on only the things I could control. When I started to think negative thoughts and emotions, I would acknowledge them and then reframe them quickly to a positive thought. Being in an unfavorable environment can be incredibly draining, so it is important to have some self-care practices in place.

Think about an exit strategy. When I stopped seeing a light at the end of the tunnel, I worked on my exit strategy, and that became my goal.

Overcoming Lack of Education

Cassobin (Cassie Velasquez and Robin O'Shea) writes: Owning a business within the field of education adds an extra layer of overcoming a fear of the lack of education. Although we both did postgraduate work in the field of education and hold multiple master's degrees and a Ph.D., we were insecure that maybe we didn't have the education needed to own the business and take it to the next level.

As a result, we found business consultants and mentors to guide us. We surrounded ourselves with professionals that have skills and knowledge that we don't have. As a result, we tripled the sales in our business in two years.

Don't hold back from regularly seeking feedback from peers and mentors. Use the feedback they give to identify areas for improvement and to adjust your learning strategies. Keep up with trends and developments in your field by reading industry blogs, news, and research papers.

Staying informed can compensate for any lack of formal education. You know the saying: It's not always what you know but who you know. Surround yourself with those who have knowledge and expertise in areas that you do not.

Jenny DeBolt writes: Sure, college is an accomplishment, but I don't believe it's necessary for everyone. Passion, perseverance, and drive can't be taught. If you have those qualities, you're already miles ahead of what formal education can offer.

Overcoming Lack of Family Support

Cassobin (Cassie Velasquez and Robin O'Shea) writes: Overcoming a lack of family support while running a business can be challenging, but it is possible. Fifteen years ago, we worked together for the company that we now own. At that time, we trained all over the country, and we were gone a minimum of two weeks a month. We both had little children at the time so having the support of our spouses was critical. We didn't, however, realize that right away. We used to joke about going on a "girls' trip" when we were going to work, and our spouses didn't find that funny as they were left to manage the household. We were having the time of our lives visiting different cities and enjoying what the city had to offer, and all the while, our spouses were at home dealing with the kids and the day-to-day life to keep our households afloat. We realized quite quickly that we needed to show empathy to them for all that they were doing for us to allow us to be on the road.

When we decided to buy the business, we knew that we needed to sit down with our families and include them in the business decisions we were making. We knew we needed to talk with them about EVERYTHING because without their support, we couldn't do it.

Weekly family meetings were put in place to check in to see how things were going and what things weren't going so well. We began to involve our spouses in all business decisions that would affect them. This has been a key factor in our success.

Jenny DeBolt writes: Many people struggle with a lack of family support, but if your family or friends don't support you, are they really the people you should be seeking approval from? Their lack of support might be holding you back. It's time to let them go. Be true to yourself and live for you!

Overcoming Feeling Judged

Amber Harman writes: The need to be perfect and the feeling of being judged, I think go hand and hand. When we feel judged we naturally want to be better or perfect. As I get older it gets easier to not let this affect every aspect of my life, but I still struggle with it, and I have a feeling I always will. I admire people who live more freely, but I was not blessed with this level of confidence.

We live in a society where we are on social media daily, and we constantly have everyone's' perfect lives in our faces. But I have to remind myself that what we see on social media is never the whole picture. It's hard to not feel judged about the things I have, the way I look, or how successful I am. What gets you through is to have supportive friends and family. I am blessed to have both, and even though it's not easy, that's what helps me get through. Having a strong support team is the key!

Cheryl James writes: When I started my business, the feeling of being judged was my constant shadow. Every move I made seemed to be scrutinized, not just by others but by my own critical inner voice. The fear of judgment often made me second-guess my decisions.

To overcome this, I had to change my mindset. I realized most people were too busy with their own lives to judge mine as harshly as I imagined. This revelation was liberating. I started focusing on my goals instead of worrying about others' thoughts. Each step forward, no matter how small, became a victory.

I also found peace in building a support network. Surrounding myself with like-minded entrepreneurs provided a safe space to share fears and triumphs. We laughed at our mistakes and celebrated our successes together. Knowing others faced the same challenges helped me feel less alone and judged.

Another tactic was to turn judgment into fuel. Instead of letting it paralyze me, I used it as motivation to prove my doubters wrong. Their skepticism became my drive to succeed. Over time, I learned that the only judgment that truly mattered was my own.

In the end, overcoming the feeling of being judged was about embracing my journey and believing in my vision. Judgment still comes and goes, but now it's a minor obstacle. Each success makes me more confident and less concerned about others' opinions.

Silvia Hernandes writes: Growing up in Brazil, where the emphasis on appearances is strong, I often felt judged if my attire didn't match perfectly. However, moving to the U.S., where there is less focus on external appearances, significantly helped me overcome this feeling of being judged.

Professionally, my journey was also challenging. As English is not my first language, I often felt more scrutinized for any linguistic mistakes. During my time at Nestle, one performance review from my boss advised me to take a typing course. Initially, I felt embarrassed, realizing that typing wasn't a skill emphasized in my cultural upbringing. Though my job performance was satisfactory, my boss desired more efficiency. I overcame this feeling of judgment by reminding myself that not everyone is adept at typing—it's a skill that can be learned.

Harboring a fear of judgment can lead to losing oneself. It takes maturity and time to embrace who you are, stand firm in your desires, and maintain your thoughts without succumbing to external judgments. What others think of me is truly none of my business.

SIX-FIGURE CHICKS

Section 3

Best Practices and Advice for Becoming a Six-Figure Chick

In this section, we are giving the best practices and advice we wish we had received early on in our journeys when we were just starting out. These are the things that helped us bring in six figures or more every year!

We've organized the advice and tips by topic, based on the type of HAT we had to wear, activity performed, strategy, and thought process. We recommend reading through them all to glean advice for all areas of business (and life!)

Goal Setting

Amber Harman writes: Setting goals is the easiest way to get to where you want to be. For me personally, setting smaller goals to cross off your list makes it easier to achieve the bigger goals. I like to make a list, and as I cross those ACHIEVEMENTS off one by one, I feel more accomplished. It's rewarding to know that you are getting things done!

Betsy LaVoie writes: "School is never out for the pro," is a quote I heard in my early adulthood that has always resonated with me. Continuously seeking motivation and inspiration to set and achieve new goals has proven successful for me. I've also learned to keep my goals private, which goes against the common advice to share them with others. I believe this depends on the individual—if telling others your goals helps keep you accountable, that can be great advice. However, I've found that I can believe in my goals and abilities more strongly than some well-meaning naysayers, who may not even realize their negative impact.

Why share your deepest goals with those who might have doubts? People's energy is contagious, and someone's doubt in your ability or goal can set you up for failure. Be true to yourself: if you set a goal that you know you can achieve and are willing to take the necessary actions, pursue it boldly and quietly. I've also learned that your own energy and subconscious mind are always "on." If you tell yourself you're going to do something, do it. If you let yourself off the hook, your subconscious may start to discount your intentions and not believe you'll follow through in the future.

Jenny DeBolt writes: Listen, comfort is the enemy of doing great things. I swear by GO BIG when it comes to goal setting. If your goal doesn't scare you, it's not enough. Go bigger.

My first year in business, I set a goal of hitting $1M. The people I shared that with either straight out told me that was nuts, or politely moved on to the next topic, avoiding talking me back to reality. While I may not have hit that in my first year, I did hit it by year two. That's pretty amazing! Year two, my goal was to grow by 50 percent, or $1.5M per year. That I hit! Then I said 50 percent again, and I grew by 60 percent!

Kimberly Mitchell writes: I've done quite a few workshops with people on SMART goals: Specific, Measurable, Achievable, Realistic and Time-bound. I think from a business perspective, having quarterly, bi-annual and annual goals are helpful. Further goals, like three-to-five-year goals are not as detailed. Writing them down and telling the appropriate people so you are held accountable is important. For the business, we have an annual revenue goal and a bi-annual goal, as well as bonuses that are paid out bi-annually and annually. Because of this, sharing each month's numbers with our admin staff is important so we're all held accountable, and we all know what's going on.

Making your goals visual helps. At the beginning of the year, I bought all the materials for my entire admin staff to make their own vision boards. I think there's something about seeing visual goals on a regular basis that helps to manifest them. Many people think about their goals, but they don't take steps that would hold them accountable because no one knows. Accountability for your goals is essential.

"A goal without a plan is just a wish."

— ANTOINE DE SAINT EXUPÉRY

Shantoya Nicole Thomas writes: I believe that goal setting is greatly important. My motto is "Dream big!" We often spend lots of time setting goals, dreaming, planning, having vision board parties and such. Yes, set the goal, but I am a big believer that what we do next is an important part of the goal. We must learn to put those goals into a plan for the next steps. This is where I often found myself stuck wasting time. This is also why I am so passionate about Six Figure Chicks and the wealth of knowledge shared when so many brilliant minds come together.

1. Set BIG GOALS! Don't play yourself small. Dream with no fear, no budget, no hesitation.
2. Be Specific! Go after what you want.
3. Be prepared to work for your goals.

Stephanie Russell writes: Goal setting as an entrepreneur is the cornerstone of turning vision into reality. It's about defining clear, actionable objectives that drive your business forward and keep you focused on what truly matters. Successful entrepreneurs break down their long-term vision into short-term, measurable goals that guide daily actions and decisions. These goals should be specific, attainable, and aligned with the broader mission of the business, allowing for flexibility as circumstances change.

By setting and regularly revisiting goals, entrepreneurs can track progress, stay motivated, and make informed adjustments to strategies. Goal setting also fosters accountability, both personally and within the team, ensuring everyone is working towards the same end. Ultimately, it's not just about setting goals, but about executing them with determination, persistence, and a willingness to adapt, turning aspirations into achievements.

Attitude of Gratitude

Amber Harman writes: Everything happens for a reason. This is my daily affirmation. I tell myself this multiple times a day. I don't know how you get through life without knowing each and every day that everything happens for a reason. Even the bad. I have dealt with the loss of loved ones and other hardships, but without those experiences I would not be where I am today. I am a firm believer that if you miss that flight, you avoided some other disaster that would have been worse.

Gratitude is a struggle for me. Of course I am grateful. I have the most amazing husband who is constantly supportive. Gratitude comes a little easier for him, and I admire it so much. How lucky am I that he is mine? I'm grateful every single day, but I also deal with the general public, and it's hard. They are experiencing the most stressful part of their day in traveling... getting to the airport, going through security, getting on their flight. I am the first person they see, and kindness seems to flee during their process of traveling. It can weigh on me. But I have to keep telling myself that it has nothing to do with me.

What I can tell you is that at the end of the day, make some time to think about how blessed you are. I see so many people, and I see their struggles. When I feel that negativity starting to sink in, I get overwhelmed knowing that I have it so good. It could always be worse. At the end of the day, I know that I have a good job, and I have lots of people who love me and care about me.

Jenny DeBolt writes: Gratitude changes lives and saves lives. Create and hone a sharp gratitude practice. About seven years ago, when I was at a low point in my life, I decided to start a gratitude practice. I'd read about the habit rule—three weeks to make, three weeks to break—and made a promise to myself to stick with it every day.

Each morning, before doing anything else, I'd write down three things I was grateful for in a journal. I'd do it again before bed, without fail. Sometimes it was something small, like 'a good hair day' or 'I got up on time.' Other times, it was something bigger, like 'my son got the job' or 'the weather was beautiful today.' The key was consistency: three things, no matter how small. And it was important to write it in my own handwriting; it speaks to your subconscious and continues to work in your mind.

While I don't keep a gratitude journal anymore, practicing daily gratitude has become second nature. In fact, one of my sons mentioned a few years back that he can't complain to me anymore because I'm always saying things like, 'Well, at least it's not...' or 'It could have been worse.' I've just naturally developed the habit of seeing something good in everything.

Shantoya Nicole Thomas writes: Having an attitude of gratitude is easy when life is going well. It's in the difficult times you have to remember to remain in an attitude of gratitude. As we go through life, we often forget the obstacles we've overcome. When climbing the ladder of success, the journey ahead becomes all we see. I often have to remind myself how grateful I am for the opportunities that are before me.

1. Be humble. To whom much is given much is required.
2. Mindfully notice things! Don't limit yourself to big or monetary things, you could be grateful for something simple like the sun

shining or air that fills your lungs.

3. Intentionally choose to feel gratitude! Be aware of both your perceived barriers and blessings, and try to balance your perspectives.

Personal Finance

Kimberly Mitchell writes: My number one rule is: Always pay yourself first! Your basic needs have to be paid first, but the second those things are covered, pay yourself. It's got to go somewhere: a savings account, the stock market, 401k, or whatever you decide for how you want to pay yourself first.

I was blessed with an entrepreneurial dad and an accountant mom, so budgeting and money knowledge was passed down to me naturally. I remember my dad getting all the stocks out of the Sunday newspaper and teaching me, keeping track of them, and having conversations about investing. As soon as I could get a credit card that I could put money on in order to spend it to build credit, I did. There were conversations about IRAs, investing and compound interest.

I have these financial conversations with my teenagers now, but unfortunately a lot of parents don't because they don't understand personal finance. Often the only time families sit down and have a conversation about money is when there's a problem. This can cause people to form a bad relationship with money. Normalize talking about it with your partner and/or children and learn together!

Shantoya Nicole Thomas writes: Oh, personal finance! This is a very personal matter indeed, but one that needs to be discussed. My first true entrepreneurial success was great. I made great money, opened multiple locations, cars and such. What I didn't do was manage finances well enough. Money in, money out was the motto. When the economy took a turn—which it did, and it will—everything and everyone attached to the business suffered. I had failed... big. I had not protected my personal finances, so there was no business. You are the first investor in your business. Your time and money hold value.

1. Personal finances can help you maintain your finances at a healthy level and reduce stress and anxiety.
2. With good personal finance management, you'll learn to control your money so you can achieve your goals.

Silvia Hernandes writes: My first piece of advice regarding personal finance is to thoroughly understand how taxes work. Many people lack tax literacy, and gaining as much knowledge as possible on this topic can significantly minimize the impact on your earnings. Delving into tax codes can reveal numerous savings opportunities.

Secondly, make saving a habit, regardless of your income level. Aim to save 10-15% of every $100 you earn. Consistently setting aside a portion of your income, no matter how small, can accumulate into a substantial amount over time. Before you know it, you could find yourself with $10K in your savings account.

Lastly, live within your means. While it's tempting to mimic a millionaire lifestyle, it's unwise to incur debt by purchasing extravagant items like a luxurious car you can't afford. Prioritize finding a reliable vehicle that suits your budget without compromising your financial stability. It's more important not to flaunt wealth unnecessarily. Instead, focus on saving money for your larger aspirations rather than for emergencies, as intentionality often shapes reality. Money should be reserved for dreams, not merely for unforeseen circumstances.

Wealth Building

Stephanie Russell writes: Wealth building as an entrepreneur is about more than just generating income—it's about creating lasting financial freedom and legacy. Unlike a traditional job, where your earnings are capped by salary or hourly wages, entrepreneurship offers the potential for unlimited growth through ownership, innovation, and strategic investment. By building a business, you create an asset that can appreciate over time, generate passive income, and provide opportunities for reinvestment.

Entrepreneurs can diversify their wealth by leveraging profits to invest in other ventures, real estate, or the stock market, compounding their financial success. The key to wealth building in entrepreneurship lies in resilience, strategic risk-taking, and continuously seeking opportunities for expansion. It's about transforming vision into value and reaping the rewards of your hard work, not just for today but for generations to come.

Hiring & Managing a Team

Cassobin (Cassie Velasquez and Robin O'Shea)

As best friends and business partners, we are a team! We also have a fabulous group of talented men and women on our team who conduct our trainings. However, we quickly realized that we needed a team of professionals on the business side of things. Hiring and managing teams effectively is crucial for the success of any business.

- Tip #1: Hire a business coach
- Tip #2: Delegate tasks and responsibilities to empower your team members to make decisions within their area of responsibility
- Tip #3: Do monthly or bi-monthly meetings with your teams. We do them by zoom and call them "Happy Hours." It is a time for the whole team to connect. Always provide an agenda beforehand and leave time for questions.
- Tip #4: Do individual "Check-Ins" with your team members. We do this twice a year. This provides a safe place to talk about what's working for them, and we also ask them if we, as the business owners, could do anything to improve their work experience.
- Tip #5: Tackle any conflicts as soon as they arise. This prevents escalation and helps to maintain a positive work environment.

Maintaining the relationships with your "peeps" is key.

Jenny DeBolt writes: Take care of people. Do it simply because it's the right thing to do. People just want to know they are loved. If I err on the side of humanity and it backfires, I can live with that. But if I err on the side of self-interest and it backfires, then maybe I deserved that—I got exactly what I put out into the world. Humans are meant to be in community, and when they feel loved and supported, there's no limit to how far they'll go for each other. It's truly a beautiful thing.

I can confidently say that if I died tomorrow, my team and staff would have nothing but positive, loving things to say about me because I genuinely care for them, and they know it. When you leave people feeling loved, they thrive. And that's what they'll remember about you. That's a beautiful emotional legacy to leave behind.

Kimberly Mylls writes: I have hired 100's of people when I was in publishing and every summer I hire a new team to run my non-profit summer camp. What I have learned is people can look great on paper, have the experience but unless they share your values, managing them will be difficult. Understanding someone's values is the first step. The second is knowing what motivates them. Is it money, recognition, collaboration, or something else? Once you know their values and what motivates them you can set clear goals. Then it comes down to communication and deciding together how you are going to communicate and what are the expectations. For example, one of my business partners wants to email, another wants to text, decide how you are going to communicate and how often. I also have a rule with everyone I work with, which is a 24-hour response or some type of acknowledgement.

Lucy Kairalla writes: Hiring and managing a team are two different things, but I'd like to focus on hiring becaukse I believe if you hire properly, managing your team will be a breeze. One of the most important things to consider when hiring is cultural fit. It's easy to focus on someone who aligns with the education, training, and experience necessary for the job title, but if you have someone who doesn't fit into the culture, you will have issues.

Business owners don't have time to deal with extra issues. These disruptions will inevitably take away from your other responsibilities. The other thing to consider is specific roles and responsibilities. Your expectations of your team need to be clear for yourself, and it's important to ensure they're aware of yours. Once you're clear about what you need and expect, you can hire someone with the knowledge and skills to get the job done well, which will free you up to do all the other things on your list.

Managing a team can be difficult, but if you learn to hire people who will complement your team and fit in with the overall culture, they will add value which will help growth and success feel more seamlessly attainable.

Scaling Strategies

Cheryl James writes: Scaling my business felt like trying to juggle flaming torches while riding a unicycle. The challenge of scaling seemed overwhelming, but I knew it was essential for growth.

To successfully scale, I started by breaking down my big vision into manageable steps. Instead of trying to scale everything at once, I focused on one area at a time. This approach made the process less daunting and allowed me to celebrate small victories along the way.

I invested in learning by attending workshops, reading books, and seeking advice from mentors who had successfully scaled their businesses. Their insights and experiences were invaluable, providing me with practical strategies and boosting my confidence. Knowledge truly is power when it comes to effective scaling.

Building a strong team was another critical strategy. I worked with people who were not just skilled but also shared my vision and passion. Delegating tasks and trusting them allowed me to focus on strategic growth rather than getting bogged down in day-to-day operations. It was a game-changer.

Implementing automation and leveraging technology played a significant role. Automating repetitive tasks and using efficient software solutions streamlined operations and improved productivity, allowing us to scale without overextending resources.

Because of the challenges I faced and the lessons I learned; I started a program to help others navigate their own scaling journeys. Through these strategies, I was able to grow my business sustainably and effectively. Now, I'm passionate about sharing these insights to support other entrepreneurs in achieving their goals.

Jenny DeBolt writes: When you're a smaller business, it can be impossible to afford a full-time team member, and you might not even have enough work to justify forty hours. Instead, consider outsourcing to established companies. You can outsource tasks like inbound calls, email and message management, scheduling, billing, accounting, taxes, administrative work, human resources, onboarding, projects, and much more. You don't have to wear all the hats. Learn to delegate and take things off your plate. Just because you can do something doesn't mean you should.

Imagine how much your business could grow if you focused solely on your core activities, rather than getting bogged down in day-to-day tasks. Let other professionals handle what you can afford to outsource. Start with offloading your least favorite tasks.

I held onto invoicing and payroll processing for far too long. The relief I felt after finally letting go of that control is indescribable. I should have done it much sooner. Learn from my mistake.

Lucy Kairalla writes: The very nature of what I do is to help companies scale their business using marketing. I often hear clients say something like, "I grew my business by word of mouth." This is great, and I'm always happy to hear about the success they've attained. But we're all in business to make money, and to make even more money we need to learn how to scale. This can be challenging, especially for those with a more risk-averse mindset.

Here is what I tell them: "You can grow without investing in marketing if you're an excellent service provider who sells an excellent product.

Your business will grow naturally. But you only have two hands, and at some point, your business will plateau."

If you're unwilling to invest in digital marketing, this tells me you're not serious about scaling your business. When you invest in digital marketing you're going to reach the masses. A best practice in the business world is to invest 11-14% of your revenue into marketing. This is a healthy and necessary number that should be thought of as an investment, not an expense.

Taking this practice seriously has helped me avoid hitting those plateaus and brick walls during my growth journey that many business owners see due to an unwillingness to invest in marketing.

Self-Care Leverage

Betsy LaVoie writes: I used to think I couldn't afford the luxuries of what many women call self-care, both in terms of time and money. Facials, manicures, massages, and hair treatments seemed like indulgences rather than necessities. However, I do believe I perform best when I look my best, so I dress the part every day—full hair, makeup, jewelry, and all—even if I'm working from home. I "suit up" regardless of the day and learned early on to dress for the position I want, not the one I have. Someone walking into the building should know at first glance who the most senior leader is.

Although I still don't spend time or money on getting my nails done, I've embraced self-care routines that provide significant benefits, far exceeding the ROI for my time and money. For example, I never had a professional facial until I was forty-six, thinking it was unnecessary when I could do it myself at home. Fast forward four years, and I now get a facial at least once a month, with additional treatments as needed. That first facial led to the esthetician discovering an abnormal spot and recommending I see a dermatologist. Two separate skin cancer lesions, thirteen weeks of radiation, chemotherapy cream, and Mohs surgery later, I'm forever grateful for my monthly facials. My esthetician isn't a doctor, but having someone regularly examine my skin with a magnifying glass and a deep knowledge of skin health has proven to be time and money well-spent. This is just one of many self-care necessities that have become priorities in my schedule, which I used to consider unaffordable.

Jenny DeBolt writes: I am a master of self-care. People often ask how I manage to do everything I do, and the answer is simple: self-care. You can accomplish a lot when you make time to take care of yourself. I carve out time for a twenty-to-forty-five-minute bath almost every day, two to four facials per month, church, Bible study, reading, yoga, time with family and friends, laughter, two to three retreats per year, two-week vacations at the lake, and so much more. The list goes on. Sure, I get tired and burned out like everyone else, but I recover quickly thanks to all the self-care I prioritize.

Networking

Ania Kubicki writes: They say your network is your net worth, and I believe it. When I started my business, joining NAWBO was a game-changer. This group didn't just help me form strategies and build connections—it taught me the true essence of networking.

First, networking is not about attending events and asking for something. The best networking happens when you show up to serve. Before attending any event, ask yourself how you can contribute. Volunteer, offer your expertise, or get involved in the organization. Giving before asking builds trust and stronger, more meaningful connections.

Second, I learned the hard way that networking isn't about joining as many groups as possible. Early on, I spread myself too thin by joining too many organizations and clubs. I was everywhere but truly present nowhere. The result? Burnout and diluted relationships. My advice: focus on no more than three networks where you can be genuinely involved and contribute consistently. Quality over quantity is key.

Networking is about creating value for others, which in turn creates value for you. By serving and staying focused, you build a network that truly enhances your net worth, both professionally and personally.

Cheryl James writes: When I embarked on my entrepreneurial journey, I quickly realized that networking was essential. Building a business can be a lonely road but connecting with others opens up countless opportunities.

At first, I was hesitant. Walking into a room full of strangers felt scary. However, I soon discovered that networking was about building genuine relationships. I attended local business events and joined masterminds, meeting people who shared similar challenges and aspirations.

One of the most significant benefits of networking was the exchange of knowledge. I learned from fellow entrepreneurs who generously shared their experiences and insights. These interactions provided practical tools and renewed confidence.

Networking also helped me find mentors who guided me through tough decisions. Their support was crucial in navigating the ups and downs of running a business. In turn, I began mentoring others, creating a cycle of support and growth.

Collaborations were another unexpected perk. Partnering with other businesses for joint ventures or cross-promoting services expanded my reach and created win-win situations. These collaborations boosted my business and fostered camaraderie.

Recognizing the impact networking had on my success, I started a program to help other entrepreneurs harness the power of connections. Networking isn't just about who you know; it's about creating a supportive ecosystem where everyone can thrive.

In essence, networking transformed my business by turning isolation into collaboration, challenges into opportunities, and acquaintances into friends.

Ginger Clayton writes: Someone once told me that it isn't who you know, it is who knows you. I am involved in various groups across different platforms. You can join women's groups, associations, chambers of commerce, business mastermind groups, board of directors, etc. Diversify the groups that you are in. I try to set a certain timeframe to stay in a group so that I can make room to try others; there is only so much time.

I would say that the biggest piece to learn is not to stay too long if it isn't the right group for you or your business. You may get other benefits from it, and that is okay too. Including one group that is specifically for sharing leads, or people in the group are asked to help make meaningful connections is important. I like boards for many reasons. If it is a non-profit board, it is great to help others while also connecting with like-minded business associates. Whether it is a nonprofit or for-profit board, you make meaningful connections by rolling up your sleeves and working side by side for the same goal.

Lisa Riley writes: I LOVE people and believe everyone has a unique story to share. However, the prospect of networking at large events used to be quite intimidating for me. Over time, I developed three strategies to ensure my time at these events was both productive and enjoyable:

1. Identify My Purpose: Before attending an event, I determine my goals. Who do I want to meet? What connections would be most beneficial for me? Having a clear purpose helps me stay focused and make meaningful connections.

2. Research: Preparation is key. I gather information about the event, the attendees, and any potential contacts I want to meet. This not only boosts my confidence but also provides conversation starters, making interactions smoother and more engaging.

3. Focus: At the event, I stay focused on my goals while remaining open to new opportunities. I prioritize meeting the people I identified beforehand but ensure I'm not dismissive of others.

Every conversation is valuable, and you never know where a casual chat might lead.

By using these strategies, I transformed my approach to networking from a daunting task into a rewarding experience. I now look forward to events, eager to learn from and connect with the diverse array of people I meet.

Stephanie Russell writes: The power of networking when building a business as an entrepreneur cannot be overstated. Networking opens doors to opportunities that would otherwise remain inaccessible, from forging strategic partnerships to finding mentors who offer invaluable guidance. It allows entrepreneurs to connect with like-minded individuals who can share resources, insights, and support. Networking also helps in building a brand's credibility and expanding its reach, as word-of-mouth recommendations often carry more weight than traditional marketing. By actively participating in industry events, engaging on social platforms, and nurturing relationships, entrepreneurs can tap into a wealth of knowledge and experience that accelerates growth. In essence, networking is not just about who you know, but about cultivating meaningful connections that can propel your business forward, foster innovation, and create lasting success.

Public Speaking

Ania Kubicki writes: Public speaking is more than a platform—it's a powerful catalyst for business growth, brand recognition, and thought leadership. I've always been passionate about it because it's not just about standing in front of an audience; it's about sharing your unique expertise and making a lasting impact.

First, recognize that your insights are worth sharing. Your experiences and knowledge bring a fresh perspective that others need to hear. As a PR professional, I used to worry that my audience already knew my content. I quickly learned that my unique take added depth to familiar strategies, offering something truly valuable.

Second, immerse yourself in the world of public speaking by listening to others, especially those in your field. Here's why:

- Expand Your Perspective: By attending talks, you gain new insights and approaches that can elevate your own presentations.
- Validate Your Message: Industry conferences showed me that even top speakers often deliver similar content to mine, reaffirming the value of my insights.

Lastly, don't shy away from unpaid speaking engagements. Exposure is invaluable, and even seasoned pros often speak pro bono to reach new audiences. Public speaking is your stage—use it to amplify your voice and influence.

Lucy Kairalla writes: Some people are natural speakers, and some are not. But whether this comes more naturally to you or not, it's a skill that can be developed even further. Expecting to step on a stage and deliver a truly inspirational speech without preparing and having a well-thought-out plan is delusional. You could get lucky once, but that won't be repeatable. If you don't put the work into the content and method for delivery, you'll never blow the minds of your audience. And isn't the point of giving a speech to inspire and move them to action?

This is the difference between a keynote speaker and those who are speaking to get leads. The preparation that happens before your speech is what will give you confidence to provide a moving experience. As a marketer, it's my business to provide as much value to my clients as possible. This doesn't stop with the services I offer. This includes supporting my target audience with as much valuable content and information as possible which will help me build their trust in me and my company. It's not about me. It's about them.

To avoid doing them a disservice by not being prepared I've invested in coaches and put time and effort into programs like Toastmasters. To become a skilled speaker it's important to practice and you have to want to be great.

Monica May-Dunn writes: Public speaking is my biggest fear, which I am now in the middle of overcoming. I'm not quite comfortable yet, but the more I do it, the better I feel. I heard Lyn Saint James speak, and she said, "Be comfortable being uncomfortable." That has definitely helped me in public speaking.

My first answer to public speaking requests would be no, but I have to get better at it, and the only way to get better and more comfortable is to do it. Any opportunity you have, when people ask you to be on a panel or talk about something, just say yes. Go into it thinking about giving instead of what you're going to get out of it. I do lots of breathwork and lots of practice beforehand. If it helps, think about the fact that people in the audience are there to hear what you have to say. They're not there to judge you. You were asked to speak because you have something valuable to say.

Work / Life Balance

Amber Harman writes: Being a flight attendant is a perfect role for a work life balance scenario. You can work as much as you want or as little as you want. I was a single mom for twelve years. I never missed anything for my son. It's hard to believe that he is sixteen now.

In my career, I never missed out on anything. The best part of a career as a flight attendant is the flexibility. I have always been able to give trips away or pick up trips. If my son had a soccer game, I could move my days and be there. I know I touched over gratitude, but here I am feeling it. I was ALWAYS there for him. If I needed to have extra income, I was able to pick up extra trips as well. There is such freedom in being able to control your schedule.

I went through a phase where I wanted out of being in the sky. I went to apply for a job that I really wanted that would keep me home every night. When I tell you I wanted this job, I *really* wanted this job. I was so stressed after the interview that she wouldn't choose me. But she did, I got the call that I got the job, and the wave of emotions hit... I was excited to know that I didn't have to travel anymore. Then realization sank in that my FLEXIBILITY was going to be gone. This job would be Monday through Friday. I started to think about all my personal trips coming up and having to ask for time off. It was a huge wakeup call to know that I do have a job that gives me the opportunity to move things around and be with my family.

Cassobin (Cassie Velasquez and Robin O'Shea) writes: Isn't this the goal of every successful woman... to find work/life balance? We can tell you that it has ebbed and flowed over the years, and we have learned some valuable lessons.

- Tip #1: Learn to Say No! I know we want to do it all, but we just can't. Know your limits and don't take on more than you can handle. We set monthly goals related to new projects and we also say to each other, "We are not taking on any new projects for three months," or whatever, just so we can get caught up on other things that get pushed aside and reset. This is critical so you don't burn out!
- Tip #2: Take care of yourself first. You can't give what you don't have. Prioritize activities that promote physical, emotional, and mental health, such as exercise, personal hobbies, and spending time with your family and friends. Getting in a workout each morning sets the tone for the day. A nice glass of wine helps too!
- Tip #3: If you have to, schedule your week ahead of time so that you ensure you are making time for yourself and also to ensure that you are not losing sight of the ones around you... your spouse and kids.
- Tip #4: Unplug. Disconnect from work emails and calls after office hours to give yourself time to relax and recharge. Consider setting specific times to check work-related messages. Build in time to watch your favorite mindless show on Netflix!

Take the time each week to manage your own schedule. If you don't, you will be like us in the beginning and find yourself working 15-hour days and forgetting what is most important... your health, your family and your friends.

Lisa Riley writes: In my twenties, I came to realize that the concept of work/life balance is a myth we've created. Life is what we are living, and we choose how to spend our time, whether it's working or playing. There have been times when I've spent sixty hours a week engrossed in work, missing out on holidays, parties, family events, and meals. There's a time for this level of dedication, but it's important to acknowledge that when I'm doing this, I'm making a conscious choice to prioritize work.

My goal is to live each day fully, recognizing that sometimes work will take precedence, other times play will, and occasionally, both can happen simultaneously. Balancing these aspects isn't about strict separation but about understanding and accepting the fluid nature of our choices. When I choose to work long hours, I am consciously deciding to focus on my career at that moment. Similarly, when I choose to spend time with family and friends, I am prioritizing my personal life.

The key is to be mindful of these choices and understand that balance doesn't mean equal time for work and play but rather an equilibrium that brings satisfaction and fulfillment in both areas. By embracing this perspective, I can navigate my days with a sense of purpose and harmony, knowing that I am actively shaping my life based on my priorities and values.

Lucy Kairalla writes: As a woman and entrepreneur, my attention and focus are constantly being challenged and stretched to the limit. There is no limitation to the number of hats we wear and roles we juggle.

I recognized how important work/life balance is, so I learned early on to delegate and create systems that would serve these needs. This helps me to be as effective and move through each day with as much grace as possible. We're not going to win every single day. More importantly, we won't feel like we've won each day. But my team feeds off my energy, and that doesn't stop when I get home.

When I'm tired, I'm more short tempered. This energy clings to me and follows me into each space as I navigate my day. My to-do list will never stop, but I can maintain some control by having established and effective systems. I take one day a week when I don't check emails or answer phone calls. It took a while to get to the point of feeling comfortable enough to do this.

This is one of the hardest things to do for a Type A personality, which is why most entrepreneurs don't take a day off. Often, we wear this busyness as a badge of honor. It's important to remember that busyness is not a synonym for success. Success for me is knowing that I can enjoy a last-minute day off on any given Tuesday with my children, knowing that my business is in capable hands with the team I built.

Utilizing Technology

Cheryl James writes: Embracing technology was a game-changer in scaling my business, and I want to share some tips that helped me along the way.

When I first started, automation became my best friend. Tools like Zapier automated repetitive tasks like email marketing and social media posting, freeing up time for strategic growth.

Investing in a robust CRM system was crucial. You want something that will manage all customer interactions in one place, making relationships smoother and more efficient.

Moving to cloud-based solutions like Google Workspace allowed flexibility to work from anywhere and collaborate in real-time. This adaptability was invaluable as my team expanded.

Data analytics became my secret weapon. Tools like Google Analytics provided insights into customer behavior, enabling informed decisions and boosting strategies.

Effective communication tools were essential. Slack and Microsoft Teams kept my team connected and productive, enhancing collaboration.

Building a strong online presence through social media management tools helped maintain consistent posting and engagement. Tracking performance across platforms became manageable.

Cybersecurity was always a priority. Using strong antivirus software, enabling multi-factor authentication, and regular updates protected my business from threats.

Project management tools like Trello and Asana keep tasks organized and ensure deadlines are met, making team collaboration seamless.

One significant lesson I learned was the importance of continuous learning. Technology is always evolving, and staying curious helped me keep up. This inspired me to start a program to help other entrepreneurs navigate their tech journeys.

Utilizing technology effectively transformed my business, making operations efficient and allowing me to focus on growth and serving clients.

Lisa Riley writes: Wow! We live in a remarkable world. Forty years ago, there were no cell phones, computers were prohibitively expensive and just emerging, cars didn't drive themselves, and cameras used film that needed developing. Today, I use all of these technologies in my daily life, and they certainly make things easier. Apps like Calendly or Bookings enable instant, mutually convenient appointment scheduling. Office calls can be forwarded to cell phones, which are also used as cameras, and are great for texting, reading, and even shopping.

However, technology cannot replace humanity. Despite all the technological advancements, a genuine conversation with another person remains priceless. Relationships are key and more vital than ever in our tech-driven world.

Silvia Hernandes writes: Technology permeates every aspect of our lives. As business owners, mastering at least the basics is imperative; otherwise, we risk stagnation. While many tasks can be delegated, possessing fundamental computer skills is essential.

Adopting new technologies and evolving your mindset are crucial steps. Resisting change will only prove detrimental. It's vital to understand and effectively use the systems integral to your business operations. Excelling in at least one primary system you frequently use can significantly enhance efficiency.

Commit to continually learning about new technologies daily. Major tasks, like website development, can be delegated, but being proficient in the small, everyday technological tasks is necessary.

Platforms such as LinkedIn Learning offer excellent courses on various systems. Additionally, Google courses, Coursera, and YouTube tutorials provide valuable insights. With AI advancements, creating personalized learning paths has become even simpler. Embracing technology is non-negotiable; it's an enduring fixture in our world.

Leadership

Kimberly Mylls writes: You have heard all the leadership cliches like lead by example, there is no "I" in team, and think outside the box. All are true to some extent, but I found the best way to lead is to surround yourself with people who are smarter, have a different skill set but who share your values. Good leaders aren't afraid to surround themselves with the best. You don't hear a leader tell someone they are overqualified because they aren't intimidated.

Good leaders know when to step in and step away. Leadership is about being able to bring out the best in others. It's important to know what motivates each individual on their team. I'm not motivated by incentives and recognition, but I know more people excel for praises over raises, so I learned to recognize and celebrate their achievements, big or small, to boost morale and motivation.

The hardest lesson in leadership I learned was that you can't motivate someone, but you can provide them with an environment that is motivating.

Collaboration and Joint Ventures

Cassobin (Cassie Velasquez and Robin O'Shea) writes: Collaboration is one of the key tenants of our training, our business, and our partnership. As best friends and business partners we value each other's expertise, talents, and perspectives. As special education teachers we were a part of a diverse team made up of the student, professionals and families. Valuing each member's expertise and input ensured the student's needs were being addressed. As business owners we operate with the same philosophy, whether it is between us or with a team of experts. When creating a successful, collaborative team keep these four tips in mind.

- Tip #1: Develop a unified vision. When all team members share the same vision, it sets a productive, positive tone where all members share responsibility for achieving the desired results.
- Tip #2: Clarify roles and responsibilities. When team members understand their role on the team and responsibilities toward action items it reduces redundancy and confusion and increases productivity, trust, and accountability.
- Tip #3: Practice effective communication. Be aware of how team members communicate and value input. It is important for you to model open communication by encouraging active participation during team meetings and individual interactions. This creates energy and builds trust.

- Tip #4: Set expectations. We call these ground rules or norms for collaboration. We review and get agreement on these at the start of every team meeting to ensure all members how to communicate effectively and respectfully as well as how decisions will be made, and conflicts resolved. Examples of our norms include, communicate clearly and listen carefully; Ask and welcome clarifying questions; Respect the view of others; Share your views willingly; Be open to the ideas and views presented; and Honor time limits and stay on task.

Community

Ginger Clayton writes: With my personal mission being to "create a fever to serve" in others, we have a lot of opportunities for community service at Elontec. We created our ElonServe program where every employee has unlimited paid community service days and is invited to join us in any of our many community events throughout the year. They include events large and small.

Here are a few examples that our team has led over the years: volunteering with AZ Diaper Bank, which I founded and house right at Elontec with a mission to provide 1M diapers annually to local families in need in need. I was once a divorced, single mom struggling and was given one package of diapers when I didn't have enough to drop off my baby at daycare so that I could go to work and my college classes. That one package of diapers has now turned into me starting this Diaper Bank, and to date we have distributed over 10M diapers.

We will stage quarterly diaper distribution orders ranging from 100,000 to 250,000 diapers typically, for the twenty-five to thirty non-profits that we serve. We have groups volunteering to help at the Special Olympics of Arizona seasonal games, food packing events for Feed My Starving Children or Kitchen on the Street. We deliver boxes monthly to schools for Kitchen on the Street of their Bags of Hope—bags filled with food for school-age children who would otherwise go hungry over the weekend/break. We held a nice Yoga for a Cause event which benefitted yoga classes for the women in prison. Kickball for a cause is a competitive and fun industry team event benefiting a local charity. We have collected items and assembled sanitary kits for our homeless veterans and also held various drives for items like diapers, period products, food, water, socks, etc. We have held movie nights in the park for a local transitional housing program. We did this on Mother's Day weekend and served chocolate-covered strawberries for the kids to give their moms, hot dogs, chips and drinks.

The list goes on and on, but I wanted to provide a variety of ideas for you to see that some are easy and small, but they make a big impact. You never know the ripple effect of helping others, like with the one package of diapers that I received and how that turned into now helping thousands of families. There are so many ideas, and there is something for everyone.

Jenny DeBolt writes: Community is one of the essences of life. Without it, humankind would wither away. We want to connect. We want to be seen. We want to be loved. Spend time truly connecting with, seeing, and loving your community. Give back, because when you give, you nourish the community.

You can give back in several ways: through your talent, time, or riches. You can also offer mentorship, share your knowledge and expertise, provide emotional support, volunteer your skills for community projects, advocate for causes, and create opportunities for others. Even small acts of kindness, like spreading positivity or connecting people within the community, can make a meaningful impact.

Be a big impact on your community. While you may feel small in what you can offer, your reach is endless. People see you giving, and it inspires them to give as well. Your actions create a ripple effect, and others will witness your leadership in this realm. Your contributions, no matter how small they may seem, can spark a movement of generosity and connection that strengthens the entire community.

Monica May-Dunn writes: I had no idea how connected the community of escrow and title and commercial real estate was until I became an owner. Phoenix is a big city, but this industry is a small world. I meet people all over through networking, and we all have friendships in common.

Helping other business owners meet people who can help them is key. When I network, it's not about what I'm going to get out of it; my focus is learning about them. I ask how and why they started their company. Then I will introduce them to people who can help their businesses grow. It's servant-leadership in a nutshell. That's what builds a strong business community and a sense of family in your work connections.

My personal family has been vital to my business success as well. Their support and understanding of my long commute (we live in Yuma, so I travel back and forth every week) makes the transitions between work and home harmonious. Being present with my family when I am home helps balance out the time I am away. Spending quality time with my grandchildren reminds me why I do what I do and what is most important.

Family

Cassobin (Cassie Velasquez and Robin O'Shea) writes: Behind any successful woman is a supportive network. Family can mean different things to different people. Family can be blood relatives; family can be your spouse and kids, or family can be your friends. No matter what, the importance of family in business can be significant and multifaceted. We couldn't have had the success we have had without the support of our family. However, for these tips, we want to focus on what we, as best friends and business partners, needed from each other to achieve our success.

- Tip #1: Trust and loyalty. We had known each other in a casual way before we both started working for the company. When we went into business together, we knew we had to put one-hundred percent trust in each other. How do you achieve this? Transparency about EVERYTHING.
- Tip #2: Shared Values. We established very early on that we shared the same work ethic but overtime, we have had to set boundaries on how we work together. We also needed to ensure that we had the same vision for where we wanted our company to go so, we set monthly and yearly goals together.
- Tip #3: Making 'best friend' time outside of business. If you are anything like us, we live, eat and breathe our work because we love it! We set aside 'best friend time,' and we agree that we are not going to talk about anything work-related. We just eat, drink and talk about all things that best friends talk about... just no work.

Being in business with your best friend is the absolute best, and we wouldn't trade it for anything!

Ginger Clayton writes: Family is the number one most important thing in my life, aside from God. We have raised five kids who are all adults now, and for the first time we are empty nesters. This is a transition and a new season in life for us. For the first time in thirty-two years, I don't have a child at home! So, we go visit them on the weekends, have family dinner and game nights often and family trips. We try to have several trips a year to our short-term rentals in Mexico, which is only three hours away, and invite the kids to come along when they can. We also plan one big family trip a year.

When the kids were all at home, we made a few things very important: a sit-down family dinner together every night without any technology, we prayed together, and all went around the table sharing our ups and downs of the day. This was sacred time together in the midst of growing our business and five kids in varying activities.

We were also blessed to have my mother-in-law living with us for ten years before she passed. This was so helpful to the whole family as she helped a great deal with the kids, shopping, meals, laundry, etc. She was an incredible baker and loved to play cards. In the last few years we were able to care for her. The same was true with my parents in the last years of their lives. In fact, my dad had dementia and moved in with us during Covid. Fortunately, I was working from home managing my business and non-profit. It was an adjustment as I also had our two youngest kids still at home and my granddaughter doing "zoom school" from my house while also caring for my dad. Once we got into a rhythm, it was a beautiful time with these four generations that I will be eternally grateful for.

Spirituality

Ginger Clayton writes: People are often nervous to share their spirituality in the workplace. Years ago, we brought all of the employees together to establish new core values showing how Elontec RAISES the bar.

- Respect: Treating our clients, the community, and our teammates with respect;
- Agility: Being responsive, adaptable, resilient and take action swiftly for our teammates, clients and the community.
- Integrity: Being honest, trustworthy and, simply, doing the right thing;
- Spirit: Being purposeful to live in a culture of vision, faith and fun;
- Excellence: We are dedicated to achieving the highest standards and consistently delivering service that provides the "WOW" factor.
- Service: Provide reliable, loyal, and quality service to each other, our clients, and the community.

We celebrate a spirit of faith—we all have to have faith in something, and we respect the diversity therein. We have had prayer groups over the years. There were years when things were tough, and there was nothing more special for me than when a group of employees would pray together for certain outcomes. Anyone was welcome to participate.

Jenny DeBolt writes: God first in everything I do. I depend on Him for everything. I've experienced some horrendous losses in my life, including an infant drowning and several suicides. For decades, I wrote off any higher power, but deep down, I always yearned for God. Even during those years, I found myself crying out to Him in times of desperate need.

In 2020, during the first month of the lockdowns, I signed up for a breathwork session on Zoom. I can't fully explain it, but I saw Jesus—no question. That experience changed everything for me. Right after the session, I started attending church, and soon after, I was baptized.

Later, I realized that He had always been by my side, patiently waiting for me during those times of loss and other life experiences. I learned that Jesus was persecuted, so why should I expect to have no trials or tribulations? Even when I was unjustly fired from my last job, He pushed me to start my own company. I didn't see it then, but I see it now. I wasn't listening when He tried to guide me before, so this time, He gave me the push I needed—just what I needed.

When you have Faith, it allows you to see what is happening and why. It answers questions for you and guides you along the way.

Leverage

Ania Kubicki writes: Leverage is about maximizing your resources—time, knowledge, and connections—to achieve greater results with less effort. In business, it's a powerful strategy that turns opportunities into exponential growth.

One way I've leveraged my expertise is through public speaking. By sharing my unique insights at industry events and conferences, I've expanded my network, established credibility, and attracted new business without directly selling. Public speaking leverages your knowledge to reach a broader audience, turning one engagement into countless opportunities.

Another key area where leverage plays a vital role is in strategic partnerships. By aligning with complementary businesses, I've accessed new customer bases, co-marketing opportunities, and shared resources, accelerating growth far beyond what I could achieve alone.

Outsourcing is also a critical form of leverage. Delegating non-core tasks to skilled professionals frees up my time to focus on strategic activities, ensuring every aspect of my business is handled efficiently and effectively.

Lastly, content repurposing allows me to maximize the impact of my work. A single blog post can become a podcast episode, social media content, or a video, engaging different audiences without additional content creation.

By leveraging your strengths, connections, and resources, you can create a ripple effect that magnifies your impact and drives sustainable growth.

Philanthropy

Cassobin (Cassie Velasquez and Robin O'Shea) writes: As members of a service industry (education), giving back to society comes naturally. As educators we committed to serving students, families and other educators. As business owners we wanted to continue this commitment and thus decided to volunteer our time, energy, and expertise to those in need.

Not only does this maintain our connection to schools and families, but it also reminds us about our "why" and strengthens our attitude of gratitude. The key for us was to consider the needs in our community and match them with our interests and talents. Some of the best experiences have been coaching families, supporting teachers, and working at pantries. Here are some tips to consider when thinking about how you can give back.

- Tip #1: Consider your talents and interests and how you would like to use them to help others.
- Tip #2: Research different organizations to ensure their values and mission matches yours.
- Tip #3: Only commit to what is reasonable for you. Overcommitting is no help to you or the organization. Give what you can afford (in time, energy or resources).
- Tip #4: Maintain balance. While giving feels great and helps others, it is likely you are inserting this with your other commitments (family, friends, work etc.).

Ginger Clayton writes: We strongly believe in donating our time, talent and treasure. We believe that this isn't something that we should do or need to do, but it is just a way of life in whatever manner you have the means to do so. We make several donations in various aspects through sponsorships, providing non-profits with our services in-kind or at cost, serving on non-profit boards of directors and making charitable contributions.

Our employees, children and friends are always invited to volunteer in several events. In fact, none of our five children can remember a time before diaper drives! I am most excited now to lead our family in what I hope will be a generational way of life in helping to manage our family Donor Advised Fund/Charitable Trust.

What's Next?

As you finish reading these pages, you may feel inspired, motivated, and ready to take action. You've been given countless insights—from shifting your mindset, reflecting on your journey, and refining your marketing strategies to rethinking how you manage your finances and best practices. But what comes next?

The truth is entrepreneurship is a challenging path. Many falter not because they lack talent or drive but because they don't have the support, mentorship, or knowledge to navigate the complexities of building a successful, sustainable business.

At Six-Figure Chicks, Phoenix, we understand these challenges intimately. We've walked the path, faced the obstacles, and come out on the other side stronger and wiser. And now, our mission is to celebrate determined women like you who strive to overcome adversity and achieve financial success.

Do you have a challenge that wasn't addressed in these chapters? Are you seeking advice or guidance on how to tackle a specific issue in your business? Don't hesitate to reach out to the authors of this book. We are here to support you, to guide you, and to help you achieve the success you deserve.

The women who share their stories in this book have reached six figures—not by chance but through hard work, perseverance, and the wisdom gained from their experiences. They know what it takes to overcome obstacles and grow beyond six figures and are ready to share their insights with you.

Our vision is to broaden Six-Figure Chicks' reputation as a trusted publication and brand, expanding to new cities and capturing the inspiring success stories of women from all walks of life. With each story, we aim to inspire the next generation of girls and women to believe in themselves and realize the success that lies within them.

Remember, you have the power to create the life you want. Don't let fear or doubt hold you back. Take it one step at a time and know that you can do this. We believe in you, and we are here to help you every step of the way.

You can do this!

About the Author

MEL CARR, CEO AND FOUNDER OF CLOVERSY.COM, AN EXECUTIVE VIRTUAL ASSISTANT COMPANY, AND FOUNDER & VISIONARY OF SIX-FIGURE CHICKS

"I spend my time listening, seeking new perspectives, and learning more about myself and others. I'm all about embracing beauty, meaning, and purpose, and I love pushing past my limits to connect with what's out there beyond the ordinary. My life is fueled by gratitude, a good sense of humor, and knowing when to let go of things I can't control. I find joy in discovering new ideas and engaging with the mysteries that life throws at us. Through Cloversy and Six-Figure Chicks, I'm passionate about giving back to other women—helping them find their voices, crush their goals, and build lives they love."

– Mel Carr, Founder & CEO of Cloversy.com
& TheSixFigureChicks.com

Interested in Becoming One of the Authors in an Upcoming Book of Ours?

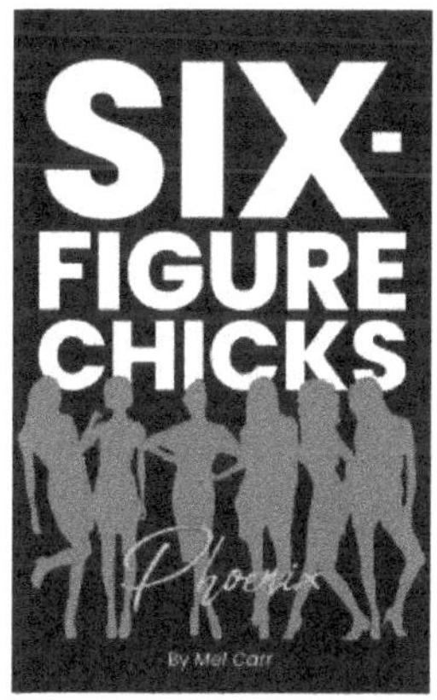

Being an author sets you apart from others in your industry and it impresses your clients! Writing one chapter in a compilation book like this one is much faster and easier than writing an entire book yourself. It's great to have your own full book, but being in a compilation book or two or three is a great place to start. Plus, all the authors share and promote the book too, giving you more visibility in many markets.

Get on our email list to be first to hear when we do this again at TheSixFigureChicks.com.

Thank You to Our Sponsors

The Adventures of Julie Jones
Live your best life NOW!

www.juliejones.biz
Motivational Speaker ~ Coach ~ Author ~
TV Show & Podcast Host

Cloversy

www.cloversy.com
US-Based Executive Virtual Assistant Agency
Do What You Do Best, Outsource The Rest!

tw | Touchstone Wealth

www.touchstonewealth.com
Fee-based financial advisory firm that provides guidance to help individuals, families, and businesses reach their goals

Brighter View FOUNDATION

www.brighterviewfoundation.org
positively impact life for people with intellectual, developmental and cognitive disabilities, seniors

US U CLEANING
No one outcleans US

www.uscleaningsolutions.com
Provides professional commercial cleaning services tailored to meet the needs of businesses.

SUICIDE & Sequins
A Journey of Joyous Hope

www.suicideandsequins.com
help others learn to cope w/ the trauma of suicide loss & to come to peace w/ suicide

CSCM
Concierge Senior Care Management

www.seniorcareofaz.com
Provides personalized, professional assessments & services to deliver effective health care for individuals & families.

KEY 2ED

www.key2ed.com
Education Administration Special Education Programs

ANGLES COMMUNICATIONS

www.anglespr.com
Strategic communications. Public Relations. Media. Events.

Made in USA - Kendallville, IN
97786_9798987198513
10.24.2024 2058